ENJOYING GOD

Enjoying God
Alan J. Niebergal

All scripture quotations, unless otherwise indicated, are taken from the English Standard Version of the Bible, copyright@ 2001,2008,2016 by Crossway, a publishing ministry of Good News Publishers.

Scripture quotations marked NKJV are from the New King James Version of the Bible, copyright@ 1979,1980,1982 by Thomas Nelson Inc.

ISBN 978-965-578-017-8

Enjoying God

Prayer and Spiritual Formation

Alan Niebergal

Contents

To the man who was Christlike at a worksite.

PREFACE

"If anyone thirsts, let him come to me and drink. Whoever believes in me, as the Scripture has said, 'Out of his heart will flow rivers of living water" (John 7:37-38).

If anyone thirsts. We all thirst. If a person doesn't drink water, they will perish. We must be replenished with water to survive. Likewise, if a person doesn't drink spiritual water, they will not be sustained. We all must keep refreshed, or we will die. Spiritually, we will also miss out on God's fullness for us. The way to fulness is in the quality of our relationship with the Lord and this quality of the relationship is in Jesus Christ and is developed in prayer. The greater our closeness to the Lord, the more fulness we will have in our life. "It can truly be said that we cannot live the Christian life unless we learn how to pray."[1]

We can choose to drink living waters, or we can drink contaminated waters that will make us sick and if we continue to drink this water, will bring death. In a country like Israel, where Jesus lived, water was precious because of the desert-like conditions in many areas. Water that stagnates is likely to carry a lot of contaminants and diseases. Water that is moving aerates itself and purifies itself. Jesus offers us rivers of living waters.

We all have a sense of incompleteness, an emptiness that we seek to fill. There are many ways that people seek to fill it—with family, friends, fame, accomplishments, wealth, possessions, recognition, sex, drugs, and a search for pleasure and comfort, power, and security in many other ways, to name a few. The result is that we live in a culture of addictions. The cry of human nature is –just a little more—just a little more of what doesn't satisfy, compared to what does. It is like trying to eat snow instead of water. Eating snow for survival can lead to hypothermia and dehydration. It can lead to death. Only pride would hinder someone from not receiving the living water, and try to find another way to sustain life or find fulness in life.

We thirst and the way we seek to fill this thirst is of utmost importance? No wonder there are so many self-help books. These wisdom ideas may assist in living a better life to a certain extent, but they don't fill man's ultimate thirst. We may have our wagon attached to the wrong star and, in the end only find the in the end emptiness, even though many people courageous their lives. Jesus said he will show us the way to fulfillment and that it is in him. He said, "I came that they may have life and have it abundantly" (John 10:10). He gives us spiritual life right now and eternal life to come, plus the result of spiritual life is fullness in this life.

In my life, I recognized strength in some Christians that I worked with and I knew, that I didn't have that strength they had and I wanted it. After seeing that strength in a few people, I read the Bible almost completely through, over the course of a year, before I prayed the sinner's prayer at the invitation of an evangelist sermon in a church and was remarkably reborn in Jesus Christ by the Holy Spirit. I wept profusely with an attitude of gratitude for his love mixed with tears of repentance as God poured his waves of love upon me. The emptiness and lack of purpose that I sensed before were now gone. I experienced peace, forgiveness, joy, and love. The overall intensity of that experience lasted about a few days. Fortunately, I had some people to walk alongside me and assist me in my discipleship in Christ. Then I had to learn to walk more by faith rather than just feelings. This is the standard for every disciple of Jesus, many may only sense that intensity for a short time, sometimes a few hours, a day, or a week. The experience of salvation may be different, but the road of discipleship is similar for all. We must learn to walk by faith and not just seek him for the feelings we receive from him, but to seek him for Himself. This is the only way to true Christian maturity.

Quite a few years after that I remember as a Pastor reading the above scripture on the rivers of living water again and thinking-- you know, I am not really experiencing what Jesus is talking about here. As a Pastor, the church was growing and people were coming to saving faith, but this wasn't bringing the fulfillment that Jesus had said would occur. Why wasn't I experiencing the fullness of these rivers of living water, even though I was walking in faith and serving Him?

The thirst is not filled in anything but Christ. Not in Christian service, not in being recognized and appreciated, in nothing but in Him. Oftentimes, our motives are corrupted and our goals contaminated. There must be a purification process that has to occur in our soul and when our wagon is on the wrong path, it will not happen. This process of the Christian life is called spiritual formation and through this process, God looks at us and we invite him to look at the deepest recesses of our hearts and cleanse these aspects of our soul so that our thirst is truly filled in Christ. It cannot be satisfied with contaminated water. The cup must be cleansed to hold the living water in its fulness. It is spiritual transformation into actual and practical Christlikeness. Not just on the outside, but deep within the heart and soul. "For the Lord sees not as man sees: man looks on the outward appearance, but the Lord looks at the heart" (1 Samuel 16:7). We must advance in our interior life.

Spiritual formation has been largely neglected in many evangelical churches and denominations. This is mostly true in local churches. This is somewhat surprising since spiritual formation is of utmost importance in the discipleship process. However, a lot of seminaries that train pastors now have a spiritual formation element. We can clean up the outside like the Pharisees in Jesus' day, but in our service to God, we can be self-serving. God's objective is fullness in our lives. (Ephesians 3:19) Not just a superficial cleaning of the outside. Our heart must be purified if we are going to quench the thirst and this thirst is quenched only in enjoying God and being in full union with him. The greater the practical union with Christ, the greater the fulfillment. (2 Corinthians 9:6) The greater our seeking of primarily God's glory the greater our fulfillment and the fuller our enjoyment of God as His kingdom is advanced.

INTRODUCTION

"Blessed are those who hunger and thirst for righteousness, for they shall be filled" (Matthew 5:6).

Mankind's greatest inmost desire is for God. Only God can fulfill man's longing, only God can complete man, and only in God does man find his home—his ultimate place of belonging. C.S. Lewis, in his books *Mere Christianity* and *Weight of Glory,* said that it *wasn't* primarily the intellectual rationale for God that brought him to salvation in Christ, but in getting in touch, with this innermost longing in his heart for God and at various times experiencing this longing and the fulfillment he experienced during the short intervals of time. These longings for God, for Lewis, were very beautiful. Reason can only take us so far. We don't know everything but God does. God's reason unlike man's is not corrupted by pride and self-seeking. Let us trust Him who knows far more than we can think or imagine.

All people at some time experience these longings. It is being drawn to something very good and awesomely beautiful. It is being drawn to the light, as the gospel of John emphasizes. We sense then a drawing to come to completion—a drawing to come home, to where we belong. As the Bible says, "He has made every-thing beautiful in its time. Also, He has put eternity into man's heart" (Ecclesiastes 3:11). God is the author of these longings.

Is it fair that God gave us this longing? If we desire goodness and wholeness, we desire God. He is God and He made us. It is a drawing to wholeness and fullness. He absolutely knows what is good and he is the essence of goodness. Yes, it is fair because he draws us to goodness which is fullness and is what is best for us and others. He extends His love to all. He created us with a thirst for what is good and He is unfathomably good and His goodness makes the most sense. Where else could we go? We can allow ourselves to be drawn to good or evil. Fulfillment is found nowhere else but in Christ. God created us for a growing love relationship with Him. However, many spend their time in countless distractions to deny these longings and try to find fulfillment in themselves, or in power, security, sex, or vanity. Mankind shoots for the wrong target and too often hits it. (Romans 3:23) Why focus on what does not satisfy? The answer is that, just like Adam and Eve, mankind looks for what they think will satisfy primarily from looking at outward appearances. However, it is a sign of health when a person longs for right-eousness, which is God himself. He is the only one righteous. (Romans 3:10) We long for goodness, as we long for heaven, a world without evil, pain, and destruction. A place of fulness and joy.

It is also very beautiful that God longs for us. He longs for us to experience the best, which is full union with Him in love. After Jesus told his followers that He is actually the bread they are looking for, in other words, he was not the way to primarily gain material things, but the very essence of life in himself, many fringe followers chose no longer to follow him. Jesus said to the disciples, "Do you want to go away as well? Simon Peter answered him, "Lord, to whom shall we go? You have the words of life" (John 6:66-68). They were catching the essence. There is no fulfillment found anywhere else. Are we truly a disciple of Jesus or just a tourist for a time, to try to get what we think we think we want? It is too easy to have misplaced affections.

We as Christians often talk about the love of God for us and how that changes us and strengthens us, however, we don't talk enough about our growing love for God and with God and of God. Loving God is what thoroughly changes us and deals with the root issues of our lives. We focus much on loving self, but are we loving self too much? To keep this in perspective, we must love God more than self, or self itself becomes an idol, to be worshiped and adored. We need a certain amount of self-love, but too much is called selfishness or, at the worst, narcissism. Without some self-love, we would not even seek true fulfillment in God or seek the salvation of our souls. However, our culture today encourages and celebrates narcissism.[1] We must love God more than self, to be ordered rightly. Jesus asked Peter during his ascension and appearances to the disciples, "Simon, Son of Jonah, do you love Me more than these?" (John 21:15). Do you love me more than the world or the things of the world? Do you love me more than other people? Do you love me more than self? Loving God is the only way to healing and to finding and enjoying our true self in Christ and to fullness in life and life eternal in heaven.

We have made secondary things of first importance and first things of secondary importance. If we have the wrong target, it is likely we will hit it and miss out on the fulness of this life, and in the life to come. If we are going to realize our ultimate goal, the goal must be very clear in our minds and heart. "If we don't know where we are going, any road will get us there."[2] What is the primary goal of man? What is the primary goal of the Christian? To answer this question is of utmost importance. In this book, I hope to emphasize not only our primary objective but also the Biblical basis and explain some of how to arrive at this goal. However, the process is so very vast and has been so neglected, especially among us as Evangelicals, that it will take another book or the reading of other books to understand the process more completely. Because it is so profound and mysterious when we let

God be God, Saint John of the Cross said that it was trying to explain the unexplainable. I will be only touching the fringe of the garment, in relation to the process. Of course, our best teacher is God, and we learn by spending much time in prayer with God and making a lot of room for God in our lives. We only learn prayer by praying. In our prayer life, we go from talking at God to talking with God, to learning how God speaks to our heart and mind and frees our will. Most of all we learn to be silent and sit or stand or walk in his presence. We need to learn how to listen to Him and fully enjoy Him. How can we grow in our love for God, if we don't regularly spend quality and valuable time with Him in prayer? Our best time should be spent with Him.

Satan doesn't want us to spend time with God in prayer and will seek in every way to get us to forsake this in our Christian life. Be prepared for resistance and press on. ((James 4:7) When we go to pray, Satan will especially seek to distract us. Everything that we could possibly imagine will be thrown into our minds and hearts. "We must never underestimate the perverting power of the demonic." [3] Prayer takes practice and persistence. We think that prayer should just be easy and natural. It is once we are proficient, but even then, we will experience different times of resistance.

We can make petitions of God when we ask God for help, support, and for things and we can pray intercessory prayers for others' salvation and assistance and healing, but the prayer we are talking about mostly is being silent in God's presence with an atti-tude of loving divine attentiveness toward God. This way, God can speak to our souls and lead us progressively into the way of fullness. This is when we are inclined to listen. When the eastern monks used to pray at times, they would repeat the "Jesus' prayer." "Lord, Jesus Christ, Son of God, have mercy on me, a sinner." Just sit, stand, kneel or prostrate yourself on the floor and quietly enjoy being with God and he will direct you. To center on God and practice a divine attentiveness to Him is to pray. It is good to remember in this learning process that a technique must never take the place of God.

We become what we desire the most. If we desire God passionately, we will become like Him, as we go progressively proceed along this road our hearts will be progressively purified. This does call for courage and integrity. Not many, however, take this road, because it is not easy. As Jesus said, "For the gate is narrow and the way is hard that leads to life, and those who find it are few" (Matthew 7:14). This road takes the utmost devotion, diligence, and perseverance. It is a rigorous journey, but well worth it. The closer you are drawn close to God, the more you will be drawn like a magnet to God. The more you are drawn to God, the more obstructions are removed, and the greater the fulfillment, the closer to the pure essence of goodness you enter into with God. As John of the Cross said, "The soul, then, enkindled with the love of God, yearns for the fulfillment and perfection of love in order to have complete refreshment therein. As a servant, wearied by the summer heat, longs for the refreshing shade, and as a hireling awaits the end of his work, the soul awaits the end of hers."[4]

One of the people in history, who had been very Christlike was Francis of Assisi. Many say that he was the most Christlike person in this modern era. His influence even today is enormous. He has inspired and directed many by His absolute passion for God. Thousands were drawn to be with him, as he directed them to God. The dedication of these followers of Christ was radical and profoundly impactful throughout the centuries and even today. There were many others throughout history that we can also learn from and be inspired to draw very close to God. To name another passionate lover of Christ is Saint Antony of the Desert, who in the third century had hundreds come to him in the desert to be guided and learn from him the gospel and the way of spiritual formation in Christ. When we are truly Christlike, people are drawn to the Jesus we know. (Acts 4:13) At the same time, we must realize that "a holy life, though important is no replacement for gospel proclamation to the lost."[5] Along these lines, J.I. Packer states, "The way to tell whether, in fact, you are evangelizing is not to ask whether conversions are known to have resulted from your witness. It is to ask whether you are faithfully making know the gospel message."[6] Even Francis of Assisi with humility and boldness preached the gospel message enthusiastically and explained in his preaching and one-to-one evangelism, both heaven, and hell. He was a fiery preacher of the gospel on the streets.

To state it more Theologically, our ultimate goal is union with God in heart, mind, and practice. Too often, we think that just knowing about God and studying about Him will bring us to fulfillment. But even if we could understand all mysteries, if our heart is not purified and transformed, and drawn close to God, there is something missing. (1 Corinthians 13:2) If I have not a growth in my love for God—I have nothing. Of course, loving God will also result in loving others in a Godly way. We must go from just knowing God to loving God. Even in our activism, we can sense that we are not experiencing the living waters that Jesus promised. (John 7:38) It is all about Jesus.

Unfortunately, many in our Evangelical churches have reverted to just enduring life until Jesus comes, they are worldly enough to be accepted by the world, but not ever radically changed within and have given up on spiritual formation, and have settled to accepting the status quo of appearances, and seeking the approval of others, even over our approval of Jesus and love for him.

Too often, people are fooled into an approach to life as Christians where they want to put as little as possible into their relationship with God and still get as many benefits as possible and have some assurance of salvation. They want to put in as little effort and still love the world and its comforts rather than Christ and the cross of Christ. "To accept Christ is to shoulder the cross."[7] It is the way of love. One day everyone will realize how much we missed out on and how foolish we were. The relationship with God and its quality is the only thing that brings lasting fulfillment in this life and reward in the next. (Ephesians 3:19) We deny the false life of selfishness and pick up the true life in Christ. The frustration that many Christians experience is largely due to trying to live their life without Christ flowing through them. (Galatians 2:20) Just like Theology, Spiritual Formation is difficult and many only just play around on the edges.

The main problem we have as people in general and even as Christians is sinful pride, both natural and spiritual, but many do not know how to change it. Only in Christ is change possible. Satan has us running in circles when the world is dying and going to hell. "Who will deliver me from this body of death?" (Romans 7:24) "The power of evil perverts the good. "The demonic is present under a thousand disguises."[8] Pride, ingratitude, and anger, as well as all the seven deadly sins, must be rooted out in our souls and this is only done in Christ and in cooperation with Christ and by Christ. This most often is a long process. Inner sin will not be completely and utterly eliminated in this life, but we can, in Christ, be transformed and our hearts more filled with God rather than with sinful pride and self. Our reach will always exceed our grasp until we are in heaven and then although we will still have a lot of room for growth, in heaven we be without the presence of sin, that does not mean that we are fully mature, or know everything. There will still be much to learn and experience in heaven. (Romans 7:25-8:11) However, perhaps our hearts can be filled in this life to the top with Christ, as many of the spiritual giants of history, and take that inheritance to heaven with us.

Our heart is the essence of our desires. It is the essence of who we are. "Keep your heart with all diligence, for out of it spring the issues of life" (Proverbs 4:23). Our hearts have to do with our true desires—our primary desires. We come to Christ through our minds, hearts, and will. Some, however, after salvation neglect the heart. Real conversion occurs when our heart is affected, like Jonathan Edwards, states in his book, *Religious Affections*, states. However, we are called to grow in our affectionate love for God. Our desires can be set free in Christ, as we passionately yearn for Him and at the same time experience great contentment and fullness. Our emotions can be set in the right order in the true process of spiritual formation. In the process, we will also be touched with God's heart for the lost and for His church—His people.

It is imperative that we have sound doctrine and especially teach and preach the reformed understanding of justification by faith, for it is the beginning of all in salvation as well as our sanctification. What we have neglected to its full extent, is our practical sanctification which is the main aspect of spiritual formation, especially as it relates to the interior life. On this doctrine of justification by faith alone by grace alone, through Christ alone, the church or individual stands or fails. However, we have enlarged the head and neglected the heart. "The heart has its reason, which are quite unknown to the head," Pascal stated. Both are equally important, although, Theology assists us in discerning all experiences. If experiences are contrary to the Bible, it is from the wrong spirit. All experiences must be tested against scripture because Satan often pretends to be God and gives even religious direction that is wrong or wrongly interpreted or tries to lead us to implement it, with the wrong timing. We must also learn the art of discernment as well as the discernment of spirits. (1 Corinthians 12:10) Because of the misunderstanding and the vastness of the process and the difficulty, we have neglected discernment and been scared off of spiritual formation, because Satan seeks to distort and misconstrue truth. Let us go on to the fulness of Christ. "To know the love of Christ that *surpasses knowledge*; that you may be filled with all the *fullness of God*" (Ephesians 3:19).

If we do not have the target in focus, we are going to miss the mark. Some make evangelism the main focus of the Christian life. This is very important but not the primary goal. This is the fruit of abiding in Christ, but it is not the primary goal. Again, we are making secondary things first. Some believe that ministry is the primary target of the Christian life. After all, people are hurting and people feel good when ministering to others. Jesus did say, if you love Me, "feed My sheep" (John 21:17). If we love Him, we will feed His sheep. Love for the Lord is primary. (Revelation 2:4) Out of the overflow of a love relationship with Him, we will feed

His sheep. Gregory Palamas said it is "very, very dangerous to talk about God if you don't know how to talk to Him." When we love the Lord not only with our mind but our heart, we will especially feed His sheep—not only Christians but those who are pre-Christian. It will be because we love the Lord, not because we primarily want to feel good about ourselves, that we feed the sheep. Even preachers can serve God, primarily because it makes them feel good about themselves. It is good that work is done for the Lord, but it is even better if it is done largely out of love of God and with God. (Philippians 1:15-18; Philippians 1:15-18) Having said all this, the primary focus of the gospel is regeneration, not transformation. Transformation is the result of regeneration.

Regeneration is about coming to saving faith, being born again, and having been given a new heart and orientation in Christ Jesus. In Christian maturity, we primarily seek God himself, not just his benefits. Transformation or spiritual formation is accessing all the spiritual inheritance that is ours in Christ. (Ephesians 1:3) Too often Christians begin the Christian life by the grace of God and His regenerating power and then go back to walking in our own strength or living trying to earn God's favor.

Unfortunately, the Evangelical church largely has made man the focus. We are all about our needs and wants. We want to use God as a miracle-working God at demand. Some want to dictate to Him and try to manipulate Him for their own advantage. This is a sad state of affairs. We think God is here to assist us to be successful and happy, not that we are here for us to glorify, honor and love Him and to be Godly. We will be happy when we are holy. However, the road to holiness is the road less traveled. We need to redirect our gaze to the unfathomable God and seek primarily His will, rather than our own will and His glory rather than our own glory. "Spiritual joy depends on the cross. Unless we deny ourselves, we will find ourselves in everything and that is misery. As soon as we begin to deny ourselves, out of love for God, we begin to find God, at least obscurely. Since God is our joy, our joy is proportioned to our self-denial, for the love of God.

I say our self-denial for the love of God because there are people who deny themselves for the love of themselves."[9] We deny the old man and live in the new man in Christ.

The Bible defines sin as missing the mark. We don't want to be in eternity and realize that we missed the mark. Those without Christ will have missed the general main target area and will spend their time in hell, those in Christ who have missed the main goal after justification will greatly miss out in this life and on the rewards in the next. (2 John 8)

A target shooter wants to hit the mark. Our target or goal is to be Christlike as the Bible states, "For whom He foreknew, He also predestined to be conformed to the image of His Son" (Romans 8:29). We are predestined to be Christlike. To miss this mark is a great tragedy. This is God's purpose for us. However, even being Christlike is secondary. Our first target is God Himself and our love for Him. Out of a passionate longing for God that is acted upon and nourished, we will be Christlike. Therefore, our first goal is God and union with him. Out of this objective, we will experience abundant life (John 10:10) and bear fruit to His glory. Let not the desired benefit be the main goal, but let us keep Jesus as the main goal and the benefits follow. Let us keep the main person the main thing. It is all about Him and us in Him and He is us. "Which is Christ in you the hope of glory" (Colossians 1:27). God himself is our goal. Let's explore how to get very close to God. (James 4:8)

PART ONE

MANKIND'S
ULTIMATE CALLING

CHAPTER 1

FULL UNION WITH GOD IN CHRIST

"How my heart yearns within me!" (Job 19:27)

To be a Christian means to be a "little Christs." It is to be the Christ ones. It means we are like Christ. It is to be Christ-like. We don't just stop at having our outward behavior changed in Christ, we are to have our hearts radically changed as well. Our identity is fully in Christ. This, however, is a process and we must deliberately participate in this process with God, after being born again. Yes, when we are born again, we are given a new heart, positionally in Christ and experientially, but it needs to be fully lived out practically. (Ezekiel 36:26; Philippians 2:12) It doesn't just happen automatically. We can, however, participate in this work of God, through prayer, with integrity and vulnerability. "He is a discerner of the thoughts and intents of the heart" (Hebrews 4:12). Our motives must be re-ordered in Him. Our desires must come in line with our true selves in Christ, not our false selves of the flesh. (Romans 13:14; Galatians 5:16; Ephesians 2:3; Philippians 3:3; 1 John 2:16) Our passions must be ordered by Him. We

3

become our true selves in Christ, not our despised self or an illusionary self, but our true self. A self is not disordered and contaminated by sin and inordinate self-love but the self we were created to be in the fullness of the image of God.

Well, you might say, "I thought it was from my mind all the issues flowed?" (Romans 12:1) Yes and no. Our heart has to do with what we desire. If we desire God in our utmost being, we will have our hearts purified as we spend time with Him. With our minds, we choose in the power of God to co-operate with God in the process of spiritual formation. Of course, our minds are also transformed by the right doctrine applied—the right thinking of truth. What we most desire is who we are in Christ. That is our identity and character. We direct our minds to God, but we must not stop there, our minds must affect our hearts. The Longest Journey is from the head to the heart. Our heart is only changed progressively by God as we learn to be before Him in love. In this process, we will grow in self-knowledge, which will lead to being open to the fullness of Christ in you, as we agree with God. As Augustine said, "Let me know myself, Lord, and I will know you."[1] John Calvin emphasized in his writing that the knowledge of God and self are interconnected. We primarily learn about ourselves through God.

"It was this quality of love that motivated Abraham in the Old Testament to be willing to sacrifice his son Isaac to God. Abraham trusted in God's absolute goodness, even when he did not fully understand it. "He considered that God was able to raise him from the dead, from which, figuratively speaking, he did receive him back" (Hebrews 11:19) "This heightened consciousness of God's love, which makes us willing to sacrifice everything to him, also gives us a willingness to know God and to be known by him. It is what the medieval contemplatives called *affectus*, the dominant desire to know and be known by God, regardless of the cost."[2] Of course, our Theological knowledge and our Spiritual Theology or knowledge of spiritual formation must have maturity so that we can have discernment, for Satan loves to come as an angel of light. (2 Corinthians 11:14) We need to be discerning of God's leading and the leading that comes from the evil one and or the Biblical term called the flesh. The flesh is the indwelling sin that is tainted with man's original nature. It is that desire to make life work without God. To be our own God.

Our ultimate goal as Christians is to be in increasing union with Him which will result in becoming more Christlike. "(We) Are being transformed into the same image from glory to glory, just as by the Spirit of the Lord' (2 Corinthians 3:18). We are to fully participate in Christ. We are to be "partakers of the divine nature" (2 Peter 1:4). It is "no longer I who live, but Christ lives in me" (Galatians 2:20). God receives glory when we are our true selves in Christ. We do not cease to exist, but we find completeness in the full image of God in which we were created. The new self is re-ordered, the more we can live in our true selves in Christ. As the Apostle Paul states, "We know our old self (or old man as NKJV states) was crucified with him in order that the body of sin might be brought to nothing, so that we may no longer be enslaved to sin" (Romans 6:6). Provision was made on the cross, but it must be implemented. Christian, be who you are called to be in Christ. "To put off your old self, which belongs to your former manner of life and is corrupt through deceitful desires, and to be renewed in the spirit of your minds, and to put on the new self, created after the likeness of God in true righteousness and holiness" (Ephesians 4:22-24).

We are not to be *primarily* human doings; we are human beings and out of our being in Christ, we will bear fruit. "By this, My Father is glorified, that you bear much fruit" (John 15:5). You may ask, what is the fruit we will bear? Is it that other people are

influenced to become Christians, or is it the fruit of the Spirit—
love, joy, peace, longsuffering, kindness, goodness, faithfulness,
gentleness, self-control? (Galatians 5:22) It is both. It is loving our
Christian brother and non-Christian friend as Jesus said; "By this,
all will know that you are My disciples if you have a love for one
another" (John 13:35). This is especially true for our Christian
brothers and sisters. If this is happening in a church, Christ will
be lifted up. (John 3:14; 12:32) This all flows out of abiding in
Him. It also includes social justice and assisting the poor? These
are all the fruit of growing in our love for Him.

Let us not get secondary things first. The more Christlike we
become, the more we bring glory to our Triune God. Our primary
calling as Christians is to be holy, not only in justification but in
practical sanctification. (1 Peter 1:16) As God says in his word, "I
am the Lord who sanctifies them" (Leviticus 22:16). The more
Christlike we become, the more we will be drawn to God and the
more we will bear fruit. This is what it means to abide in Him.
(John 15:7) The more we increase in union with God, the more
we will enjoy Him and therefore live in Him. Others will also be
inspired to know Christ and become like Him. The greatest thing
we can do is inspire others to love, God and that comes out of our
passionate love of God. "You shall be witnesses to Me in
Jerusalem, and in Judea and Samaria, and to the end of the earth"
(Acts 1:8). What people need most is our real holiness and that
they might see Jesus in us and be drawn to Him. When the
Sanhedrin had heard Peter and John, they "perceived that they
were uneducated and untrained men, they marveled. And they
realized that they had been with Jesus" (Acts 4:13). When we have
been with Jesus and are growing in our union in Him, we will also
point others to Christ and we will proclaim the gospel by our life
and words.

CHAPTER 2

A SAINT-ONE WHO IS IN
CHRIST

"Be holy, for I am holy" (1 Peter 1:16).

Martin Luther said he was a Saint and a sinner. However, the Bible refers to all real Christians as Saints, but even saints sin. There is still indwelling sin in a Christian (Romans 7:23) because we have been tainted by original sin and the Bible refers to this as the flesh. (Romans 13:14) The flesh is that strong inclination to sin. We sin in failing to love like Jesus, in our motives and actions. The saint, however, does not have his life identified with sin, but with Jesus. His overall orientation to life is Jesus, not sin, not the old self, or the world. He has been given a new nature from God a divine nature that has replaced this fallen nature. (2 Peter 1:4) However, the flesh seems to like to align with the old nature and it can seem when this happens that we are living in the old nature. The Apostle Paul addresses the Christians as saints in his various letters to the church and throughout his writing, as does the whole of the Bible. (Romans 1:7; 2 Corinthians 1:1; Ephesians 1:1; Philippians 1:1; etc.)

A Saint is one set apart to God. One set apart to be like God—holy. To be holy means to be set apart to God—dedicated to His service and devoted to him and his purposes and glory. To be a saint also means, to be pure in Christ and to becoming pure and being filled with goodness in Christ and filled with love, righteousness, and justice. Everything about God is enormously beautiful. We can never be completely like God, but we should largely reflect Him as the moon reflects the sun. We become what we love and what is our primary desire.

A saint is someone who is in Christ. Someone who is *not* in Christ is not destined for heaven, but for hell. Being in Christ is another name for being a saint. We are a saint because we are in Christ. Someone outside of Christ, no matter how virtuous, will not be able to go to heaven on their own righteousness. They would have to be perfect and have never ever sinned once in their life to go to heaven. No one enters heaven based on their own merit. No one fits that category of being without sin, except Jesus. (James 2:10) As the Bible says, our righteousness is as filthy rags. (Isaiah 64:6; NKJV)

Being "in Christ" is a major theme if not the major theme of the Apostle Paul. He also talks about Christ being in us—the hope of glory. (Colossians 1:27) There is an abundance of scriptures that talk about us being in Christ. As the Apostle Paul said in the scriptures, "Therefore if anyone is in Christ, he is a new creation" (2 Corinthians 5:17). Here are also just a few other scriptures to consider. (Romans 3:24; 1 Corinthians 15:22; Ephesians 2:6; ,2:10; Philippians 4:21; Colossians 1:4) This is very well elaborated in the classic book by James S. Stewart, *A Man in Christ.*

All born-again Christians are Saints. Of course, we will give evidence of being born again. Jesus said, "Most assuredly I say to you unless one is born again, he cannot see the kingdom of God" (John 3:3). Jesus said, "You will recognize them by their fruits (Matthew 7:16). A Christian will give evidence of his conversion from the idolization of self and sin to Christ. Our hearts will be transformed and it will reflect on the outside in how we spend our time and what we are devoted to.

Our primary desires when we are born again certainly do change, but we must nurture those desires, or like a garden not tended, it will grow weeds. Our longings must be cultivated by God, or like a vacuum space, it will be filled with something else. We don't have to do anything for weeds to develop, just neglect the garden. Many foolishly neglect the garden of their soul and reap the whirlwind. This issue of neglect also applies to finding the way to salvation, but it also applies to growing in Christlikeness or practical sanctification. Many are too double-minded to be in touch with the fulness that Christ brings. (James 4:8)

We have been sanctified and are being sanctified and will eventually be glorified in Christ. We will explore this further in the next chapter on sanctification, which is included in the chapter on the overview of the process of spiritual formation in Christ. Suffice it to say now that those who are Saints are positionally and judicially justified in Christ (justice has been satisfied in Christ on the cross by Jesus who bore the penalty of our sin) and in sanctification, but there is also a very practical side to sanctification that has largely been neglected in its full understanding by Evangelicals and that is, that we are to be made Saints practically, as it relates to deep changes within our heart that are reflected in who we are and how we live -- our motives, the basic root of ourselves. However, unless we were positionally sanctified at conversion, we would not be able to be in the presence of a Holy God. God covers us in the righteousness of Christ and puts Christ's righteousness to our account. It is righteousness not our own but given by Christ.

Even though our inheritance is freedom from sin, we still sin—whether in thought, attitude, word, omission, or sinful actions. We have not been brought to a place that is absolutely free from the presence of sin like we will be in heaven. At the core of our being, we have been given a new heart, but this heart needs to be nurtured in Christ and in prayer if we are to come to the fulness that is in Christ. Jesus said, "Blessed are those who are pure in heart" (Matthew 5:8). We will see God in this life and in absolute fulness in heaven. It was said of Moses that he knew God face to face. (Exodus 33:11) Moses had a very close relationship with God and so can we. To be close to God, we must walk in the Spirit, not in the flesh. The flesh is the orientation of life that leaves God out and tries to do it on our own and takes credit for God's common grace in their lives.

We still are affected by the influence of sin in our passions and appetites, although at the core of our being, we have been changed. We need to be purified and enter fully into the holy of holies and live there. Yes, we are new creations, but this new creation in Christ must be lived out. (2 Corinthians 5:17) We are "partakers of the divine nature" (2 Peter 1:4). The more we are partakers of the divine nature in practice, the more our hearts and minds are changed, and the more we are partakers of the divine nature, the less sin influences us or has dominion over us. The result is that we are freer and freer to be our real selves in Christ.

The Old Testament prophesies about the New Covenant that Christ will usher in. "Then I will give them one heart, and I will put a new spirit within them. I will remove the heart of stone from their flesh, and give them a heart of flesh, that they may walk in My statutes and keep My rules and obey them. And they shall be My people and I will be their God" (Ezekiel 11:19-20). God will open our hearts to be responsive to Him. We, however, must nurture this openness. This is how it was from the beginning before sin separated mankind when Adam and Eve sinned and brought spiritual and physical death to mankind. (Romans 5:12-15) They were representative of us who also have sinned. We were also under the sentence of death which is, in fact, hell in eternity, because of our sin, unless we receive by God's grace the gift of salvation in Jesus Christ. (Romans 5:12-13) We sin because we have a sinful nature and our nature can only be changed in Christ. This involves faith in Christ Jesus and repentance of sin and a turning from a love of sin to a love of God. Turning from a rebellion towards God and turning to a love of Him. (Ephesians 2:1-10)

We have been given a new heart—a heart responsive to Him and all that is good. We, however, must grow into our inheritance. We still are human, but in Christ, we are called to rise above human nature and live in his divine nature. Impossible for man, but not for God working in us, as we are available to Him. (Romans 8:13) We were never called to live the Christian life in our own strength but in Christ's. However, we can also become Saints in practice. It certainly is not just theoretical or wishful thinking. This happens when we make room, much room, a vast room in our lives for meeting with God in prayer. This doesn't occur to the casual disciple of Christ. Prayer and God's word are primarily how we present ourselves to God, although this also does involve service and ministry to others. Prayer is not primarily getting things from God, but getting close to God and staying close to God. "Prayer radically transforms broken people into new people—people newly created in God. We become *fully* the unique person that God originally created each of us to be."[1]

The Christian's identity primarily is as a Saint. If we are true to our inheritance in Christ, this is who we are. This is certainly who we are judicially in Christ. This is our inheritance. Be your real self. Be true to yourself in Christ. However, Martin Luther looked at the Christian life rightly, saying it is a life of repentance. If we want to grow close to God, we must forsake all attachments that come before Christ—even that what is good, according to God's will. The good also must be rightly ordered. We must mostly separate ourselves from every impurity by repentance and confession and cleansing by God. (1 John 1:9) Only He can purify, but we have a part in the process. For instance, all of the many ways Satan tries to hide sinful pride must be exposed and forsaken. "In this peaceful refreshment, the soul attains the rest in God it seeks, however many obstacles block its path. Countless are the seductive ways of the world, the wiles of the devil, the futile attempts we make to put the pride form, not the Christ form, at the center of our life."[2]

We will explore the weightier issues of sin as we progress—the issues of sinful pride, laziness, gluttony or greed, wrath, jealousy, envy, and lust.. These are issues of the heart. These are the root of the problem. For us to become more and more Christlike, these must be rooted out by God and by us co-operating and seeking Him with intensity and passionate desire. It is a process—a long process. It takes a lifetime and a life of prayer. "By contrast, we can now start to see that a life without prayer is probably the greatest impoverishment we can experience."[3] As Jesus said, "One thing is needful" (Luke 10:42).

Are we Saints and are we becoming Saints—are we being sanctified? If we are not becoming Saints, we are letting the weeds of the world, the flesh, and the devil crowd out what is ultimately good and is worth everything to find and we are missing out on our ultimate calling. It is also not making our calling and election sure. (2 Peter 1:10) As Leon Bloy stated, "The only real sadness, the only real failure, the only great tragedy in life, is not to become a Saint."

Of course, the Roman Catholics and the Eastern Orthodox churches pray to Saints. This certainly is not Biblical. As the Bible states, "For there is one God and one mediator between God and men, the Man Jesus Christ" (1 Timothy 2:5). Of course, the Catholics also pray to Mary, although she was a great woman and very responsive to God, it also is not Biblical to pray to her. The Roman Catholics and Eastern Orthodox honor saints, people that have lived Godly lives. It is significant that they have these as their heroes. Shouldn't these be our heroes as well? They Biblically are not, however, to be prayed to. These men and women, whom the Catholics call Saints, have usually been very Christlike and very dedicated. However, let us not, as Evangelicals, proverbially, throw out the baby with the bathwater. We can learn much from these saints, although it takes much discernment.

These people dedicated themselves to God without reservation and to a life of prayer. Many of them were monks and spent their most valuable time in prayer. Their life was a life of prayer. We learn prayer by praying and we can learn much from those who made their life a life of prayer.

Some Evangelicals might be surprised to learn that *some* Roman Catholics and Eastern Orthodox actually know the Lord. They talk about being converted rather than being born again. There are evangelical Catholics, although they would not use that term for themselves. They have come to experience Jesus in saving faith. They come to the Lord in spite of a distorted Theology that emphasizes their own merit and efforts to obtain their salvation, instead of justification by faith alone as the reformers like Martin Luther and Calvin taught, although they may come to a heart understanding of justification by faith alone. Catholics believe in justification by faith plus merit. One must be aware of this in reading the saints. In fact, one must be well grounded in Theology to sort the wheat from the chaff, even though on the matter of spiritual theology, we can learn much from them. In fact, they have been keepers of spiritual theology for over two thousand years. Luther, Calvin, the Puritans, Quakers, Evangelicals, and Pietists have gleaned much from them.

How do the Catholics come then to the Lord in spite of some distortions in Theology? It seems that they primarily come through the assistance of the heart and the reading of God's word. They respond to the Lord speaking to their hearts. Jesus said, "Everyone who has heard and learned from the Father comes to me" (John 6:45). I know some Catholics that definitely know the Lord and some Evangelicals that have become Catholics because of the lack of depth in Evangelicals and the neglect of spiritual formation in Evangelical churches. By reading the Roman Catholic Saints such as Francis of Assisi and Sant John of the Cross and Teresa of Avila, you can definitely tell that they had a deep and close relationship with the Lord.

Many of these Saints knew the Lord and knew Him very well. They understood the workings of God in our hearts and mind and could teach it to others. Even though we must carefully sort the truth from error, we have much to learn from them as it relates to spiritual formation. They tended to believe that you merit heaven and could not know for sure you were saved until you saw Christ after you died. How sad to not have the assurance of salvation. (1 John 5:13; Romans 8:16)

We as Evangelicals are often exhorted to act a certain way, like the emphasis of the Pietist, but are not told how to become the way they are exhorted to be. This can be frustrating. That is the value of spiritual formation. It focuses on the process that God has ordained to transform us from the inside out.

Starting back in the third and fourth centuries, when the desert Fathers went to live in the desert because of the corruption of the church and the world, they passed on a great heritage to the next centuries. With these Saints and others that followed them through the centuries, we have two thousand years of learning at the feet of Jesus in prayer. These people were very committed and dedicated, taking vows of celibacy, poverty, and obedience. They spent much time in prayer. Their lives were all about prayer. They became proficient in experiencing God and being transformed by Him in His presence. We would do well to learn from them.

These people were rigorous in their dedication and commitment to the Lord and their passion for Christ inspired many and many of the Saints still inspire people. Maybe we could learn again the value of leading by inspiration. We can learn from the Saints the greatest inspiration is to be Christlike. What the people need most other than Christ is for their leaders to be truly holy, practically— not just acting politically pragmatic. Of course, we, similar to Francis of Assisi, not only inspire people to be passionately devoted to God but explain the gospel with boldness, humility, and love.

We are a saint positionally in Christ through justification and sanctification, but we are called by Him to be a saint also in practice. To not have this as our goal is to miss the mark, to forsake our primary calling and passion. (Ephesians 4:1) Our first purpose is to be in full union with Him and thus be Christlike. To have our image of God restored in Jesus Christ, not only fully in heaven but right now. "Your kingdom comes. Your will be done on earth as it is in heaven" (Matthew 6:10). As far as this is possible in this life.

However, a saint is not perfect, although he is moving towards perfection. Jesus said, "Therefore you shall be perfect, just as your Father in heaven is perfect" (Matthew 5:48). To be Christlike is not to be perfect. None but Christ have ever been perfect. This, however, is our goal in Christ and it will take an eternity. A saint is growing in closeness and thus Christlikeness. "A Saint is not a man without faults, but a man who has given himself without reserve to God," as Bishop Westcott states.[4]

CHAPTER 3

THE MISSING BLESSING

"Able to comprehend with all the saints what is the width and length and depth and height—to know the love of Christ which passes knowledge; that you may be filled with all the *fullness of God"* (Ephesians 3:19).

We, as Evangelicals, have the width and length of the Christian life, but we are largely missing the depth of the heart. In the last few decades, we are now even largely missing the width and length. We need to learn again, like Martin Luther and Calvin and others and the importance of the doctrine of Justification. We have emphasized too much the unbalanced love of God and forget that His love is couched in His justice and holiness. Without understanding justice and holiness, we can't truly understand love. As even John Wesley said, "Beware of all honey."[1] We will never understand or appreciate the good news until we understand the bad news.

We have become shallow in our Theology and as well neglected a missing dimension and that is the importance of Spiritual formation. We have focused on salvation, and forgotten its twin brother, spiritual formation. Theology is very important and absolutely essential, but we as Evangelicals have neglected what the essence of who we are is and that is experiencing God. We have neglected the best. Systematic Theology and spiritual theology should never be separated. This is similar to grace and truth—they also must never be separated. They must be held together to teach the whole counsel of the Lord. (Acts 20:27) The world has recently seemed to have forgotten about grace, let not the people of God do the same.

We, as Evangelicals, have always emphasized the importance of experiencing God in our lives, perhaps not enough about enjoying God. Having the affirmation of the Holy Spirit in our lives that guarantees our election in Christ. "The Spirit Himself bears witness with our spirit that we are children of God" (Romans 8:6). The Spirit bears witness in our hearts. (1 John 5:13)

Our focus as Evangelicals is experiencing God in salvation and in our daily life. Some like myself have had a radical and very emotional salvation experience, some people grow into a love relationship with God, but they know they are Christians because their desires have changed. These desires are for God and the work of God and they give evidence in their lives by their dedication and commitment to Christ. These are experiencing God in a love relationship. He gives us His peace. "Therefore, having been justified by faith, we have peace with God through our Lord Jesus Christ" (Romans 5:1). This peace is experienced.

Theology is important, but it should not be separate from Spiritual Theology. Both Theology and spiritual Theology or of utmost importance, other than the Lord Himself. Spiritual Theology is primarily learning by actually praying. Yes, most evangelicals pray vocal and mental prayers, which are primarily prayers of petition, intercession, or request, but we must go on to learn meditative, contemplative prayer, which is primarily where spiritual formation occurs and is learned by encountering God in silence. Contemplative prayer is the prayer of silence or, as some have explained it the prayer of the heart. This is the prayer where we primarily remain before the Lord in stillness and attentiveness to Him and let the Lord reveal Himself and us and reveal us to ourselves, as well. It results in dialogue and instruction by the Lord. As the philosopher-theologian Blaise Pascal said, "All of humanity's problems stem from man's inability to sit quietly in a room alone."

There are stages or dimensions of prayer that are only learned by practice and perseverance. There is vocal prayer, intercessory prayer, and contemplative prayer. Contemplative prayer is a gift that is given by God by His sovereign choice to those who seek Him with all their heart. It is a gift, but we can co-operate with God in receiving His gift. Sadly, many evangelicals know little or nothing of contemplative prayer. In a survey done of Evangelical pastors, the average pastor spends ten minutes in prayer a day, not counting the prayers he says on the go. This makes the pastor quite vulnerable.

Connie Rossini was asked how to practice contemplative prayer. Her answer is: "You don't. Contemplation is not something you can practice. It is a loving gaze at God, who is love. When a soul dedicates herself to prayer, especially meditation on Scripture, as well as growth in virtue, she greatly pleases God. God then—initiates—in His own time—a deeper love—communion with her. God bestows His love upon the soul and lifts her up, so that she may also gaze upon Him in love. She communes with God beyond words, concepts, and images. This is a foretaste of heaven when we will see and love God as He is. (See 1 John 3:2)"

Thomas Dubay, in his book *Fire within*, describes contemplative prayer in this way, "... a divinely given, general, nonconceptual, loving awareness of God. There are no images, no concepts, no ideas, no visions. Sometimes this awareness of God takes the form of a loving attentiveness, sometimes of a dry desire, and sometimes of a strong thirsting. None of these experiences is the result of reading or reasoning—they are given, and received. The infusion is serene and purifying. It can be delicate and brief, or in advanced stages, burning, powerful, absorbing, and prolonged.

Always it is transformative of the person, usually imperceptible and gradually but on occasion obviously and suddenly."[2] God is the great initiator in prayer. He invites us into a divine dialogue in prayer.

Spiritual Theology is about Christ being formed in us in practice. It is the process that God uses to shape us into the image. We were created to be holy and this only occurs in Christ. It is the only way the pride will actually be lessened in our lives and thus make room for God. These are stages of prayer that people who have been people of prayer have recognized and the understanding of the process and how to respond as we journey along with God, and these understandings are critical to implementing in order to reach our destination. That is, of course, if our goal is the same as God's. Besides, we will not find fulfillment anywhere else. This is where God's richest blessings are found. Our fulfillment and happiness are not the primary goals, but it is a result of drawing very close to God, as close as a person can get. Even in the midst of bearing the cross, we can find fulfillment in the Father, as did Jesus. The Christian's most complete happiness will be in heaven, but here on earth, we can experience fulfillment and joy, even in the midst of the influence of evil. This also can occur in spite of the actions and responses of other people.

As J.I. Packer once stated in an address, "The church in North America is 3,000 miles wide and half an inch deep." This relates to Theology but also, its neglected brother Spiritual Theology. In this world of instant gratification and oversimplification and thus confusion, the idea of spiritual formation seems alien to the Evangelical church. Spiritual formation takes dedicated time and diligence. In general, the modern Evangelical church has oversimplified its Theology and thus its preaching and teaching and has very little emphasis on the true gospel in the atonement of Christ and Spiritual Theology. However, all is not lost. As God said to the Ephesus church that had lost its first love, "repent to do the first works," and the Lord will restore us.

How did we neglect our first love? We will also explore that in more detail later, but suffice it to say, we have focused on the cognitive and behavioral and forgotten the heart. It is about the motives of the heart. Spiritual directors can also be helpful to assist us on the journey. We also, on this journey, need to be aware of not being overly scrupulous. Let us be clear, our first love is the Lord and here on earth, our first love is spending time with Him and that is through prayer. We don't know how to pray as we ought. It is God's work within that is important. We need to present or make ourselves available to God.

"There is a reason that people do not enter deeply into prayer. "The problem is not simply all around us, but inside us as well. So, prayer becomes a weapon that can painfully turn on us. Prayer opposes everything in us that is false, evil, and sinful. Prayer attacks all the indifference and moral complacency, all the conceit and selfishness within us. Prayer assaults our spiritual apathy and dryness. Because of this, prayer is constantly the means we can use to reassess our values and objectives before God."[3]

Satan will resist you the most in developing a life of prayer, as well as in Bible reading and study, which really go hand in hand. Prayer is the big battleground that can bring us close to God. The early disciples knew the absolutely critical importance of prayer. The early church appointed deacons to carry out some administrative duties and said, "But we will give ourselves continually to prayer and to the ministry of the word" (Acts 6:4). Some Christians would think the pastor is wasting his time if he was devoting time to prayer.

Perhaps we have forsaken this dimension because it is the hardest. "J.C. Ryle could remark: "I have come to the conclusion that the vast majority of professing Christians do not pray at all."[4] We have neglected the best and focused elsewhere. As Houston states, "In fact, one of the most prayerless spheres can be seminary or even a church. Scholarship about God, or religiosity in the name of God, can subtly become a substitute."[5] Again we have made what is secondary, primary. Leadership, management, and administration have taken prominence instead of prayer. These secondary matters are important but not primary. We also need to organize if we are going to reach the lost and disciple God's people in their walk with Jesus.

We can have a picture of someone or even a biography of that person, but if we really want to get to them, we must spend time with them. We may move to a mutual relationship with that person, and if they are especially wise, we will listen very carefully to them when they speak. Many things are caught rather than taught. We will want to know what they like, and what are their desires, and share our lives with them. Looking at a picture and perhaps even kissing the picture and saying kind words is not enough. In the same way, we can study about God, but fail to experience Him and be close to Him. This is especially true for us modern evangelicals since our focus is the Bible, which also can take the place of God. Yes, the Bible is very, very important, as, through it, God reveals Himself, but it is not to be worshiped instead of God. Jesus was born in a manger, but we do not worship the manger instead of Jesus.

Some, on the other hand, make prayer all about spiritual warfare. Certainly, spiritual warfare is a part of prayer but as the Bible says, "Therefore submit to God. Resist the devil and he will flee from you" (James 4:7). Our focus must remain on God, not the devil. The way to overcome the devil is to submit yourselves to God. We must not take our focus off our target or will become the target. We must always let Christ stand between Satan and us. However, we must also remember that as we draw close to God, we will be a target for the enemy of our soul—the devil. He will seek to hinder us or to throw us off track. Greater is he that is in us and he that is in the world. (1 John 4:4) Jesus said, "But take heart; I have over-come the world" (John 16:33)

The good news is, if we pray and make it a way of life, we will be drawn closer and closer to God and have more and more freedom from the evil one. We will be drawn to the Lord, like a flower to the light and warmth of the sun. In the Lord, we will make breakthroughs against evil and we will be transformed in Him. However, it will seem, at times, like a slow process and some strongholds will take great perseverance. (2 Corinthians 10:4-5) Do not be surprised also that you go through times of aridity and not because of blatant sin.

There is so much deception, deceit, and distortion in sin that it takes a while to wipe away before we come clean. As St. John of the Cross states, we are like a smudged window, not able to see clearly, until the window is cleaned. As the Bible says, "The heart is deceitful above all things, and desperately sick; Who can understand it? I the Lord, search the heart and test the mind, to give every man according to his ways, according to the fruit of his deeds." (Jeremiah 17:9-10). Prayer calls for integrity before Him. Integrity is in crisis in our modern society. Primarily integrity before God which leads to integrity with self and integrity before others. Self-knowledge and knowledge of God go together. This can be difficult because, as the Bible says, our hearts without Him possess no good, as the apostle Paul states in Romans 3:10-13.

"None righteous, no, not one; no one understands; no one seeks for God. All have turned aside; together, they have become worthless; no one does good, not even one." It may be difficult to admit this reality. Without knowing the love of God, we cannot face the corruption of sin within. Our self-worth is found not in ourselves but primarily in God, his goodness, and his love. When we are assured and confident of his love, we can face what needs to be transformed in us and has been marred by sin. We only need to consider the cross to be confident of God's love for us. However, many find it easy to live in an illusion rather than in the truth. The consequences are not easier.

How can a person even look at Himself, if it is so bleak? No one seeks after God. Unless God does a work in our life, we will wander in a stark wilderness and waste our lives. The world would be hell if not for God's common grace, in this world now and without his love giving us peace, purpose, and direction. God is the author and finisher of our faith as the Bible states. (Hebrews 12:2)

The more we nurture this divine nature, the more predominance Christ will have in our lives. However, we must always remember that it is the work of God. There is the passive part where we let God do the work in us and the active part in which we co-operate with Him. The wise come to discern the distinction and apply it according to God's leading. This is developed in the process of spiritual formation. It is not learned overnight.

"For the word of God is living and active, sharper than any two-edged sword, piercing even to the division of soul and of spirit, of joints and marrow, and discerning the thoughts and intentions of the heart. And no creature is hidden from His sight, but all are naked and exposed to the eyes of him to whom we must give account" (Hebrews 4:12-13). Karl Barth said, "There can be no proud Theologians." True Theologians are not only humble in their minds but in their hearts and there is a process called spiritual formation in the cleansing of the heart. The desert monk Evagrius said, 'A theologian is one who prays, and one who prays is a theologian." If we are only a Theologian of the mind, we are truly experiencing the whole or the fulfillment Jesus talked about. Notice that Jesus said, "You shall love the Lord your God with all your heart, and with all your soul and with all your mind" (Matthew 22:37) He mentions the heart first and mind last. It is also recorded this way in Luke 10:27. Luke adds the word strength after soul. The point is that Jesus emphasized the heart. Not only does our thinking need to be transformed, but so does our heart. This is the point of spiritual formation. In the West, we have emphasized the head and largely neglected the heart.

Any good that man does or becomes is attributed to God. How then is a person to receive self-esteem? When I was in school in the San Francisco area in the 80s, I noticed a book in a secular book store related to how to live an illusion as the way to happiness. At first, I thought they were joking. Now that philosophy has become mainstream.

When I graduated from a Baptist Seminary in California, a book from Robert Schuller was given to us from his organization called *Self-Esteem the New Reformation*. This book is a great distortion of the gospel, but many have sold out the gospel to inordinately feel good about themselves even though it is not established on solid ground. Many would rather believe a lie. They are people of the lie, as Scott Peck states in the title of his book. They make themselves the goal rather than Christ. Our esteem is in Christ alone.

Our identity is in Christ. Our true selves are in Christ. Our fulfillment is in Christ. If it is sought anywhere else, it is an illusion. People seem to keep that illusion up for some time, but eventually, it comes crashing down.

In prayer, we run up against ourselves. We run up against the seven deadly sins. Unless we confess the specifics of that sin and go to Christ for cleansing, those sins will continue to dominate. It may and often does take time. Rinse and repeat. "If we confess our sins, He is faithful and just to forgive us our sins and to cleanse us from all unrighteousness" (1 John 1:9). Note that He is just. He is just because justice was satisfied for those in Christ, on the cross, when he bore the penalty of those who received him as savior and Lord. He does cleanse us if we truly want to be cleansed. It cost Him much to cleanse us, therefore, we need to take sin very seriously. The more we gaze upon Him, the more we desire Him, the more we will want to be cleansed. We desire to enter that beauty in the Lord.

Children come more easily than adults to the Lord because they are people of the heart. God speaks to their conscience and their heart and mind. They are not as prone to develop as adults do, sophisticated levels of deception and illusion. They recognize the truth when it is shared. They know within what is the truth because God is working through the Holy Spirit and they haven't developed as many barriers. The gospel is so simple a child can understand it, yet we should not remain simple in our understanding. That would be foolish. God is unfathomable and there are many unfathomable depths that we can only touch the hem of His garment. If a child remained a child, we would be concerned about their development and their ability to live a full life, so if a Christian remains a child in understanding—their ability to experience fulness will be greatly hindered. "When I was a child, I spoke as a child, I thought as a child; but when I became a man, I put away childish things" (1 Corinthians 13:11). To grow in understanding, we must be real with God in prayer. As C.S. Lewis stated, "The prayer preceding all prayer is, 'May it be the real I who speaks. May it be the real Thou I speak to.'"[6]

If we want to be people of the heart, we must live a life of prayer, where we encounter God and listen to Him. Many people just have a concept of saying their prayers, but not of contemplative prayer, which is the prayer of silence and or of the heart and it is in this kind of prayer that one, listens to God and to Him by a divine attentiveness. We have neglected the best. Martin Luther said, "It is the unique privilege[7] and the chief work of Christians to pray." Luther knew the value of prayer, having been an Augustine monk before breaking free of the distortions of the Catholic church.

We are to be simple of heart, trusting in God but not simple in our Theology, both the Systematic and Spiritual are complex and God is unfathomable in His depth. In the same chapter, in verse 2 Corinthians 13, the Bible says, "And though I have the gift of prophecy, and understand all mysteries and all knowledge and have faith to remove mountains, but have not love, I am nothing." To understand mysteries is to put together the complex truth and hold it in balance. Understanding mysteries is not a bad thing, in fact, it is a good thing, but we must understand mysteries and have them combined with love. The love is primarily a love for God. Out of this love being perfected each day, we love others. Let us keep the primary focus the primary focus. Let us understand the deep things of God in the heart as well as the head.

There are deep mysteries of God, because God in his absolute fullness is unfathomable, yet we do not have blind faith. There must be room for mystery in our Theology. We don't know everything.

Our reach also intellectually is beyond our reach. We must think things through with the truth God has revealed in His word and by his spirit, but we must leave the mystery as a mystery. For instance, every facet of God's sovereignty and human responsibility as revealed in the Bible is difficult to put together, even though some claim to have it all figured out. There is an aspect of this that is beyond our grasp. We must only just be faithful to God and his word and let God be God. We are not like the Hyper-Calvinist that are passive in their evangelism, as Iain H. Murray warned about in his book, *Spurgeon vs. Hyper-Calvinism*.

Our faith is based on the evidence in the Bible, reason, and confirmations in our conscience and heart by the Holy Spirit. There is faith because we do not know everything, but we make a decision and put our faith in God based on what we do know (reason, conscience, and heart) and upon who God is as revealed in the Bible and experience. God is the one who takes the initiative and converts the heart—not we ourselves, as we respond to Him and are willing and seeking.

The scripture often talks about going on to maturity. The writer of Hebrews in the Bible says, "For though by this time you ought to be teachers you need someone to teach you again the first principles of the oracles of God: and you have come to need milk and not solid food. For everyone who partakes of only of milk is unskilled in the word of righteousness, for he is a babe. But solid food belongs to those who are full of age, that is, those who by reason of use have their senses exercised to discern both good and evil" (Hebrews 6:12-14).

Where are the brave hearts? Where are those who will stand in the gap? (Ezekiel 22:30) Let us go together to the Lord. He will meet us and transform us and make us an instrument of peace, in His hands. Christ will be lifted up and draw all men unto Himself. (John 12:32) There is a burning bush around each of us, for the Holy Spirit is here among us, therefore, let us take off our shoes for where we stand, is Holy ground, and let us pray, encountering afresh the living God. (Exodus 3:5)

We have largely neglected a critical dimension of the Christian life. Let us reclaim our inheritance. Let us hold both Theology and Spiritual Theology together forever united as the closest of friends. Let us go deep in the Lord. This is our calling. He is so beautiful and he is worth it all. This is what heaven will be—being in God's presence—the beauty, power, and love of Him in His absolute goodness. As Clark Pinnock stated, "What happens on earth affects what happens in heaven."

Chapter 4

Our Heritage

"**G**iving thanks to the Father who has qualified us to be partakers of the inheritance of the saints in the light" (Colossians 1:12)

Our inheritance is in being and becoming a Saint. The inheritance we have in Jesus is in heaven as well as here on earth. Our identity is wrapped up in Christ, who is holy and it is He, that is in us. If we are in Christ, we can become holy in practice. His will for us is to be Saints, not only judicially in Christ, but in practice by being progressively transformed in Christ. "In whom also we have obtained an inheritance, being predestined according to the purpose of Him who works all things according to the counsel of His will" (Ephesians 1:11).

We can sell our birthright or we can walk in our inheritance. Esau sold his inheritance because of his fleshly desires. (Hebrews 12:16) We are talking about the inheritance in this life, in Christ. Yes, we also have a great inheritance in heaven yet to come. "To an inheritance incorruptible and undefiled and that does not fade away, reserved in heaven for you" (1 Peter 1:4). However, our primary calling now is to be Saints on earth. This will make a difference here and, in the life to come. We are primarily called to a love relationship with the Triune God. We are to be who we are called to be. "I, therefore, the prisoner of the Lord, beseech you to have a walk in a *manner worthy of the calling* to which you were called" (Ephesians 4:1). If we are to honor Christ and walk with gratitude and appreciation, we will become Saints with all our might as God works in us. As the Apostle Paul states in the Bible, "Or do you presume on the riches of his kindness and forbearance and patience, not knowing that God's kindness is meant to lead you to repentance" (Romans 2:4). We must deliberately and passionately make room for God in our lives and let Him expand this room in us. (Isaiah 54:2-3)

Too often, we sell our birthright like Esau in the Bible. (Genesis 25:31) We sell it for immediate gratification and pleasure and earthly security, comfort, or power, rather than setting our hearts on what is most valuable and that will bring the greatest fulfillment. We would rather have entertainment than making an effort to seek God with all our heart, mind, soul, and strength. Everything worthwhile takes effort, great effort. Do we truly waste time that can never be reclaimed? Life is short and then you die. Many saints not only prayed that they would live well but, when it came time to die, that they would die well. The reason that you see many pictures of saints, especially in the Eastern Orthodox tradition, with human skulls amidst the picture is that this was to remind them that life is short and they were to redeem the time as the scripture states. "Making the best use of the time, because the days are evil" (Ephesians 5:16).

"Giving thanks to the Father who has qualified you to share in the inheritance of the saints in light" (Colossians 1:12). We are partakers of the life of Christ within. He wants to separate us from sin, without and within. Sin leads to destruction, emptiness, and foolishness. Christ leads to life and life abundantly. (John 10:10) The reason that many are not experiencing abundant life is that their ultimate goal is off the mark and therefore, they do not make every effort to present their lives to God in prayer, service, honor, and love.

As Evangelicals, we have a great inheritance. How did we as a group neglect so much? If you talk to most Evangelicals about Spiritual Formation, they will not know what you are talking about. This is very unfortunate. How did we get so far from our roots?

We have made too much of the cognitive and behavioral and have neglected the heart. We are seeking to live the Christian life mostly by the will, rather than the spirit. The Christian life can never be lived in our own strength. We are told that we should be like Christ, but the process is not taught. We need to dig again the old wells. We must come back to our roots for our own health and the sake of other Christians and the world.

As Evangelicals, our roots go back to the beginning in Genesis and most completely in Christ and the early apostles, disciples, and church. We then have 2000 years of experience and instruction of Saints walking with God to draw on. Enoch and Elijah had such a close relationship with the Lord that they went to heaven without dying. (Genesis 5:24;2 Kings 2:11) Since Protestants separated from Catholics and the Eastern Orthodox in 1517, there has been some animosity between them, to say the least. In reaction to some of the distortions of Roman Catholic Theology, we have over-reacted and thrown out what is very valuable and part of our essence and heritage, which is the depth of experiencing God and being close to him. Not everything about the Roman Catholic church is bad. If any Christian group has emphasized dedication to prayer and a life of prayer, it is the Catholics and Eastern Orthodox. We also agree with them on some important convictions like The Deity and humanity of Christ, the virgin birth, the Trinity, that Christ died on the cross for sinners, the substitutionary atonement, and that He rose from the dead to give life and salvation, heaven and hell, and He is coming again in judgment and restoration.

Martin Luther and Calvin also emphasized prayer and spiritual formation. He knew the value of holding Theology and Spiritual Theology as close friends. John Calvin, in his Institutes of Christian Religion, writes in the context of the mystics and often quotes from them. One better understands Calvin if he understands the mystical context in which he wrote.

Martin Luther learned the value of prayer as an Augustine monk and the various aspects and processes of prayer. The well-known Martin Luther reads, "I have so much to do today that I'm going to need to spend three hours in prayer in order to be able to get it all done." Martin Luther knew the value of prayer and said it was as important as breathing. He would have to really enjoy and value time spent with God to spend three hours in the morning before he started his busy day.

Some would say, "How can anyone spend three hours in prayer? I can hardly spend 10 minutes in prayer." You would really have to enjoy God to spend this amount of time each day. This is learned over time. Again, it is not all about saying your prayers or just petitionary prayer although that is a part of it. It is about staying before Him in contemplative prayer or the prayer of contemplation where God speaks to your heart and to your mind through your heart. "To walk the contemplative road is to recognize that Christ alone can satisfy our longings; everything else is empty in comparison."[1] As with most things, contemplative prayer is hard at the beginning but does become more natural the longer one stays before the Lord in prayer. The closer we draw to God, the more we value the time spent with Him. However, it can take years to be proficient. There will also be times of great aridity. Do not be surprised by this. There is much enjoyment in being close to God like there will be in heaven.

If we read St. John of Cross, he was addressing monks that had already been practicing the basics of a life of prayer for some time and were living in monasteries totally committed to the Christ-life. He addresses them as beginners. These people were living in monasteries and had made vows and followed a rule of life that helped them implement a large part of their lives to prayer. He was speaking to them as beginners, in stark contrast to Christians today. He was assisting these dedicated people in understanding the whole process of spiritual formation by and with God.

Even John Calvin emphasized the importance of spiritual formation. "It may surprise some, including Calvinists, that Calvin considered "deification"—the most perfect participation in God by grace possible for a creature— "the greatest thing conceivable."[2] Deification is to become like God in the highest form possible. It is about experiencing full union with God, although still remaining who you are. It is about God being large in our lives. John Calvin's primary focus, like others, for the Christian theologically was Union with God, not just Theologically but experientially. This is how God is glorified. Deification was the highest form of union with God. This is the process where two flames become one, but we still remain distinct people. (Galatians 2:20) He understood deification somewhat differently from the Eastern Orthodox's and Catholics' conception of it. It is finding our true selves in complete union with God in practice.

Some Catholic and Eastern Orthodox speak about union with God, saying as did Athanasius, "God became man that man might become God." This is a Theological shortcut. They did, however, mean becoming deified, in grace, not in essence. However, we don't become God in grace or in essence. We can, however, become fully united in Christ. Calvin uses the term deification to mean to fully participate in the divine nature. This is to be in a state of fully participating in as complete fullness in the divine nature, as is as possible in this life. It is a realized experiential union. We never, in the process, lose our personhood, but we become our true selves in Christ. As Maximus, the Confessor states, "As a prize for ascending to God, inherits God Himself."[3]

Even the Puritans emphasized spiritual formation in prayer. However, because they did not instruct the next generation on the process, it was largely lost. Their precision in Theology was not taught in spiritual formation, they largely took it for granted.

They encouraged others to be holy but did not instruct others on how to be holy. "Our forefathers, the Puritans, in many respects enjoyed a vital spiritual life. Yet some scholars suggest that Puritan spirituality died out as a cultural force because the contemplative remained undeveloped in the movement."[4] "James Houston stated that Puritanism collapsed, at least in part, because it did not give greater attention to contemplation. He contends the Puritan Spirituality, "might have been a richer more sustained spirituality if the contemplative life had, "been more fully considered."[5] The Puritans were greatly influenced by contemplative prayer and practiced and wrote about it. Consider one of the best examples, Isaac Ambrose and his book, "Looking to Jesus." As a pastor, he would spend a month in spring in solitude in prayer. We should take this to heart today. Largely this balance between heart, mind, and will in a life of prayer among Evangelicals has been lost from the 18 to the 20th century. That is 200 years, no wonder it is so hard to reclaim. "Pascal was committed to the careful integration of head and heart. If we submit everything to reason, our religion will be left with nothing mysterious or supernatural. If we offend the principles of reason, our religion will be absurd and ridiculous." (#173)

Fortunately, in the 17 Century, we had people like George Whitefield, Wesley, Jonathan Edwards, and Brainard. Whitefield and John and Charles Wesley began the Holy Club, where they took spiritual formation and devotion, and service to Christ very seriously. These also emphasized becoming Christlike and prayer. The focus was on becoming holy in practice. They were to practice both the active and contemplative life. This was the time of the First Great Awakening. Some think it was the only great awakening in North America and that it was fully God-centered rather than man-centered. There have been other revivals and spiritual awakenings in various parts of North America, but not another spiritual awakening of this quality. As the result of this awakening, many were soundly converted and society, at large, was transformed as well as the church.

Since the 1970's spiritual formation has been slowly creeping back into our Evangelical Theological schools. As Tom Schwanda states, "There are promising signs that more Reformed and Evangelical are embracing a contemplative piety today."[6] Reformed Theologians such as Herman Bavinck have also written extensively about the contemplative element in our life in Christ and our full union with him. "For Bavinck, unio Mystica is central to his theology."[7] "Bavinck also asserts that the mystical union is the primary means for imitating Christ."[8] Now some seminaries have an emphasis both on the head and heart. One needs to carefully consider which seminary they will attend because the school you choose will help to have a great impact on a life. They must not only be solid Theologically but also as it relates to spiritual Formation. Some Catholic schools have a year focused on prayer and spiritual formation, before beginning their Theological studies. This is a wise approach. However, many attend seminaries, and their prayer lives wane. People that leave the Seminary should have good Theological knowledge but often do not have a vital prayer life.

We have sold our birthright for clever marketing schemes and shallow Theology to attract the masses and for what God can do for us and principles to follow to have a successful life. After all, God is here to serve us. Where is God in all of this? Where is a life of prayer and being transformed by God through Him in prayer? Are we truly becoming Christlike, or do sinful pride and ingratitude have predominance? Will all that we have done simply be burned as stubble as the Bible states, "For no one can lay a foundation other than that which is laid, which is Jesus Christ. Now if anyone builds on the foundation with gold, silver, precious stones, wood, hay, straw, --each one's s work will become manifest; for the Day will disclose it, because it will be revealed by fire; and the fire will test what sort of work each one has done. If the work that anyone has built on the foundation survives, he will receive a reward. If anyone's works are burned up, he will suffer loss, though he himself will be saved, but only as through fire.

work which he has built on endures, he will receive a reward. If anyone's work is burned, he will suffer loss; but he himself will be saved, yet so as through fire" (1 Corinthians 3:11-15). If we are serving God for ourselves, it will be burned up. If we are serving God for His glory and because of His love, it will last forever. Isn't it all about Jesus? Unfortunately, often we make it about ourselves and feeling good about ourselves, even before glorifying Him. Isn't it about Him and His transforming power and grace?

Often, we as Evangelicals think that Sanctification almost happens automatically or occurs instantly. We may go to a church meeting and get zapped by the Spirit and thus become more Christlike and have power for Christian service. Some, times getting zapped can happen, but the Christian life is more of a process of becoming Christlike and it is because we deliberately present our lives before God in prayer. This requires devotion and discipline and this is the way God has ordained it. We grow amidst the struggle. Just as we watch a baby learn to walk, we cannot do it for them. It is hard to watch them struggle, but this is the only way they will learn. "Love of God cannot be gained without a vigorous struggle, a persevering warfare against ourselves."[9] Too often, how we live has to do primarily, with sinful pride and ego. The definition of ego is "Easing God Out."

We need to practice an active receptivity to God. We must make room for God and that means spending quality time spent with Him focused on Him and not on what we primarily have to do that day. People are busy these days with what is less important and their business helps them to think they are important. "The Desert Fathers spoke of busyness as "moral laziness." Busyness can also be an addictive drug, which is why its victims are increasingly referred to as "workaholics." Busyness acts to repress our inner fears and personal anxieties as we scramble to achieve an enviable image to display to others. We become "outward" people, obsessed with how we appear, rather than "inward" people, reflecting on the meaning of our lives."[10]

We have our priorities all wrong. Workaholics consider it a virtue to be busy and they are honored in our society. We have made secondary matters the main concern. As the old joke goes, "When Jesus returns, looks busy." When we get to heaven, we will realize that we had it wrong and then it will be too late. We will not have remorse or guilt or abiding regret, but we will have learned that we could have so much more. More of what is of utmost value. We need to simplify our life so we can make God, much more of the priority.[11]

Many in our society think fame and fortune will bring them the satisfaction they are looking for. However, too often, the story does not end well. What they thought was the goal was only an illusion. They have set their sails for the wrong course and ended up in a barren land, stuck on a sand bar. The consequences of worshipping a false god finally catch up with us. Yet, it seems it is an illusion everyone wants to achieve. Surely the applause of men will make them feel good about themselves—even though it is short-term? However, it is only the presence of God in this life and the life to come that will bring fulfillment and ultimate happiness. As Kenneth Chafin has said, "If you don't like worship, you better not go to heaven."

"Come, everyone who thirsts, come to the waters; and he who has no money, come, buy and eat! Come, buy wine and milk without money and without price. Why do you spend your money for that which is not bread, and your labor for what does not satisfy? Listen diligently to me, and eat what is good, and let your soul delight yourself in rich food. Incline your ear, and come to me, hear, that your soul may live; And I will make an everlasting covenant." (Isaiah 55:1-3).

As the psalms said, "As the deer pants for the flowing streams, so pant my soul for you, O God. My soul thirsts for God for the living God" (Psalms 42:1-2). We must take time and effort to get in touch with this longing. Our world is filled with distractions and distractions are one of Satan's greatest tools. He wants to get our focus off of what will truly bring us fullness and life. This longing for goodness must be diligently nurtured. When it is, we will also experience this longing and fulness at the same time. They will learn to stay still in God's presence and be silent at times. (Zachariah 2:13)

Every true Christian is a saint, but not every Christian is very saintly. Some are saintlier than others. All Christians will give some evidence of being a saint. (Matthew 7:16) A saint will have a desire for God. They will hunger and thirst after righteousness. The orientation of their heart has been changed. (John 3:3) They have experienced fullness, why then would they turn back to emptiness?

Every Christian has an enhanced longing for God that they have acted upon. How much effort they put into nurturing that longing will determine the amount of fruit or Christlikeness and closeness they have in their relationship to God. Suppose they give God the dregs of their life, that is what they will reap. If they give God their best, likewise, that is what they will experience. As the scriptures tell us, "Do not be deceived, God is not mocked; for whatever a man sows, that he will also **reap**" (Galatians 6:7).

St. John of the Cross wrote an excellent book called The *Ascent of Mount Carmel.* In the book, he describes spiritual formation as an analogy to that of climbing a mountain. As we ascend the Mountain, we are more purified in heart and draw closer to God. First, it is a descent from above and then it is our response to God's descent to us. His drawing of us to Him.

If you are just going for an easy hike around the base of the great mountain, it might be quite easy. For some people, that is all they want. We get what we want. This shows how much value we place in the objective. For rock climbers, it takes a different kind of dedication. These people will not be carrying a lot of unnecessary weight. St. John of the Cross, along these lines, talks about leaving our attachments behind if we are going to take serious climbing the mountain of full union with God. Attachments can be anything that stands in our way of advancing up the mountain to our objective, which is God himself.

Freestyle rock climbers that climb without ropes the highest and most difficult mountains in the world are few. Some of the greatest say one of the appeals of this kind of climbing is the intensity of focus they must have—they can't really think about anything else and they love the challenge. They have an intensity of focus. Those who climb past 8,000 miters enter what is called the death zone. Here they will need oxygen, although there are some climbers that climb in these zones without oxygen, though it takes a lot of time to recover from these climbs. Spiritual climbers learn to walk in God and his strength rather than their own. Their absolute receptivity to God gives them supernatural strength within. The same is true of those who are passionate about God. They have an intense focus. Of course, this doesn't mean that they neglect their other responsibilities and relationship, but this first passion drives them.

The Roman Catholics think of saints as people that have attained great heights in their spiritual formation in the Lord. They are very Godly and they reflect in a great way the attitude and temperament of Jesus. They have been practically and greatly sanctified in their heart and in their actions. In their presence, you sense God and are drawn to God.

Some people in the world blame the way other Christians are for the lack of devotion to Jesus. No matter how saintly a person is—none are perfect. The closer we draw to God, the more we realize that. Some are more imperfect than others. However, blaming others for you not becoming what you expect of others to be will hold no water on judgment day. There will be no excuses for not being Christ's disciple. We have the Bible—God's revelation to mankind, we have a conscience, given by God, we have intuition given by God and we have the Holy Spirit drawing all people to the truth, to life, and fulness. If we are not a good steward of these resources, we will give an account one day. (Matthew 12:36)

If we don't put in the time, here we will likely be making up time in eternity and in heaven and we will not have the benefit of advancing amidst the sin in the world and within. Even in heaven, there will be much to learn. God in his depth is unfathomable and God has a plan for us to experience fulness.

PART TWO

THE PROCESS OF SPIRITUAL FORMATION

CHAPTER 5

SANCTIFICATION POSITIONALLY AND PRACTICALLY IN CHRIST

"Now may the God of peace Himself sanctify you completely; and may whole spirit, soul, and body be preserved blameless at the coming of the Lord Jesus Christ"
(2 Thessalonians 5:23).

Too many Christians think that at salvation, they have arrived and that they only now have to wait around or put in time until heaven. Even more unfortunate is that some who become Christians or think they are Christians get their ticket to heaven afterward but, by in large live for themselves. Like the world, it is all about them and they expect God to give them what they want, rather than what they need. Their primary focus is themselves rather than God. They have little concern for knowing God and His will, rather they would like to primary tell God their will.

Why is there among Christians so much pride, ingratitude, vanity, greed, lust, envy, jealousy, wrath, and anger among those who are called by His name? Is it because we have not taken seriously the need for the interior life to be transformed into Christ-likeness? Often times Christians take a stand in service to Christ which may

43

involve evangelism or ministry and then pull back when the devil harasses them.

When we were justified by grace through faith at salvation, we were justified and sanctified and will one day will be glorified. As the scripture states, "And such were some of you. But you were washed, but you were sanctified, but you were justified in the name of the Lord Jesus and by the Spirit of our God" (1 Corinthians 6:11). Our justification and sanctification are linked together as 1 Corinthians 6:11 states, "But you were washed, but you were sanctified, but you were justified in the name of the Lord Jesus and by the Spirit of our Lord." Because we were sancti-fied in Christ at salvation, we can stand and commune with a holy God, for he covers us with the righteousness of Christ and on his account, and thus we can be in a loving relationship with him. What now is important for every Christian is the quality of that relationship with the Lord.

If we come to saving faith our life will change. We will give evidence of our salvation. He will take our heart of stone and give us a heart of flesh, responsive to God and his love. (Ezekiel 36:25-29) If someone says they are a Christian and they don't give evidence of it, something is seriously wrong. Somehow, they haven't fully connected yet.[1] Perhaps they have trusted in their own righteousness rather than in Christ and his righteousness to save them. (Luke 5:30-32) If we are Christians, our desires will be for God and His will for our life and we will desire others too might find this great salvation as well. As writer of Hebrews says, "How shall we escape if we neglect such a great salvation" (Hebrews 2:3)

The word 'sanctify' basically has two meanings. It means first to set aside for God and His glorification. It also means to be cleansed or be made holy. "The Greek verb form for "sanctified" means to set apart for God; as a noun, the word describes a thing of person that has been devoted to the possession or service of God."[2]

We have been judicially or positionally made holy that we might be in fellowship with a holy God. We have been given a new heart and it changes us, not only outwardly but inwardly. (1 Corinthians 5:17) However, this inward transformation must be fully realized practically. This is a very important process. Because it is hard, many neglect it. However, our inheritance is complete sanctification in practice.

We are positionally sanctified in Christ and out of this inheritance, it is possible that we can be actually sanctified in practice. Too often, Christians stop at the outward life and miss what is critically important—the fulness of the inward life. Christians can be living a virtuous life outwardly and active life in service, but inwardly be perishing. As Molinas stated, "This is the way of beginners! Experience has shown that many believers, even after 50 years of this external exercise, are void of God. They are also full of themselves, having nothing of the true spiritual man except the name."[3]

Progressive sanctification is something, by in large, as mentioned previously that has been missing from Evangelical teaching. When we are talking about progressive sanctification, we are primarily talking about the interior life, not just the gaining of knowledge (doctrine), even this is also very important. Yes, our outward life needs to be morally outstanding, but it is possible to clean up the outside but be like a dead man's bones within. Jesus said to the Pharisees of his day, "Woe to you, scribes and Pharisees, hypocrites! For you, clean the outside of the cup and the plate, but inside they are full of greed and self-indulgence. You blind Pharisee! First, clean the inside of the cup and the plate, so that the outside also may be clean. "Woe to you, scribes and Pharisees, hypocrites! For you are like whitewashed tombs, which outwardly appear beautiful, but within are full of dead people's bones and all uncleanness. So, you also outwardly appear righteous to others, but within you are full of hypocrisy and lawlessness" (Matthew 23:25-28

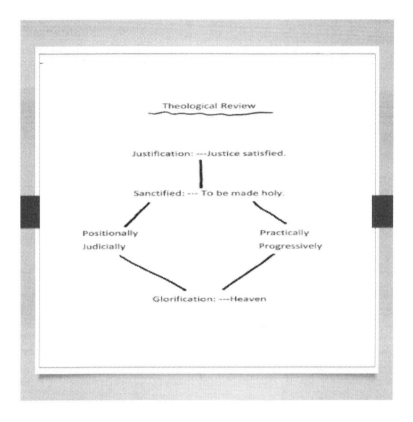

Too often, people do not sin only because they do not have the opportunity. Their hearts may be longing for sin, but they just don't have the occasion. For many of us, if we were famous or wealthy, it would be the worst thing for us. All our corruption would be focused on ourselves and exposed and we would be filled with pride. "For the love of money is the root of all kinds of evil, for which some have strayed from the faith in their greediness and pierced themselves through with many sorrows" (1 Timothy 6:10).

"Fallen men thought Christians cannot long be surrounded by popularity and success without the special help of God. 'Our God takes care always to have security that, if he works a great work by us, we shall not appropriate the glory of it to ourselves. He brings us down lower and lower in our own esteem... Some trumpets are so stuffed with self that God cannot blow through them.' You may rest quite certain that if God honors any man in public, he takes him aside privately, and flogs him well, otherwise, he would get elevated and proud, and God will not have that. Many a man has been elevated until his brain has grown dizzy, and he has fallen to his destruction. He who is to be made to stand securely in a high place has need to be put through sharp affliction. More men are destroyed by prosperity and success than by affliction and apparent failure."[4]

We have an inheritance in Christ to be transformed into Christlikeness, but we must actualize it. We must work it out in our lives. As the scriptures say, "Work out your own salvation with fear and trembling" (Philippians 2:12). We must be transformed within, by a work of the Holy Spirit. We must co-operate with God in the process. We must have a very good receptivity and docility to God. We must desire him above all. As an expert on St. John of the Cross said, "If you want to live perfectly united to God, then God can be your only goal."[5]

The Christian life is more than just behavioral and moral change, although this is part of it, it is transformation, as Jesus stated above, primarily from the inside out. This involves devotion and discipline for it to be actualized by God and His grace in our lives. This means we rise above our human nature and more fully participate in divine nature.

We must co-operate with God and seek for Him to transform us from the seven deadly sins of pride, sloth, lust, jealousy, envy, gluttony, and wrath. As the gospel of John states, the light overcomes the darkness. As we draw near to the light, sin will be exposed first and then cleansed as we co-operate with God in confessing sin and forsaking it. We need to confess the particulars of that sin. His beauty and love will draw us along, past these sins that no man can be cleansed of, except by the power of Christ. The more we are drawn to the light, the more the darkness dissolves.

He intends for us to be transformed within so that we are like Christ. "If we have been taken up into Christ, given the Spirit of sonship, the Father expects us to bear some family resemblance. He expects us to relate to all men as He Himself does."[6] We must nurture this longing for God with all our strength if this is to occur in fulness. Let us get away from the idea that it just occurs automatically. Let us be good stewards of the grace of God available to us and not, as the scripture states, not use God's grace in vain as the world. (1 Corinthians 15:10) The world uses God amidst God's common grace today, but one day will give an account. "Every knee will bow" (Romans 14:11).

Some theologians think that man is tripartite—spirit, soul, and body. Others believe that man is bipartite or has two primary dimensions—spirit and soul are one and the body is the second. The scripture also says, "For the word of God is living and powerful, and sharper than any two-edged sword, piercing even to the division of soul and spirit, and of joints and marrow and is a discerner of the thought and intents of the heart" (Hebrews 4:12). Note the focus on intents of the heart—the motives. These motives must be cleansed and reordered. Here we can make a fine distinction between spirit and soul and joints and marrow in the body. Here the writer is emphasizing a fine distinction. God's word examines our life, every fine dimension. This is necessary if we are to truly turn from disorder to order in Christ. We must be sanctified in the finest dimensions of our life. We may think some things are small things, but God often does not.

I lean toward believing that man is bipartite or has two dimensions—soul and body. The Spirit is holy it is entirely from God and is God within. If we did not have a spirit, our soul would not be alive but in salvation, God gives us a new spirit. (Ezekiel 11:19) Our soul is to be more possessed by Holy Spirit than with the flesh or human nature. Our soul can be filled with Spirit, or it will be filled with the flesh. We can be primarily partakers of the divine nature or primarily be partakers of the flesh. The Spirit is part of the soul. "Now if anyone does not have the Spirit of Christ, he is not His" (Romans 8:9).

This is where it gets even more technical. Those who go to hell because they have not chosen Christ have a soul. The soul is eternal. The soul will live eternally in heaven or hell. We can have eternal life or eternal death as our inheritance. In this life, though without Christ, people are physically alive but not spiritually alive. People are truly alive only in Christ. The soul in this world has somewhat of a connection to God, being created in God's image, and in this world, there is what Theologians call common grace. However, not everyone is truly alive. If our soul has in it the Holy Spirit, it is truly alive. The non-Christian has a spirit that sustains life but does not give them spiritual life until they receive Jesus Christ as their Savior and Lord. In hell, people will be alive in awareness in eternity but dead spiritually. "And I will give them one heart, and a new spirit I will put within them" (Ezekiel 11:19). God puts a new spirit in us when we are born again.

We are transformed into Christlikeness as we journey towards union with our Triune God in fullness. "To the measure of the stature of the *fullness of Christ*" (Ephesians 4:12). It will be well worth the effort and it will progressively become more and more beautiful. The life of prayer and being absorbed into the Divine union with God is "a heavenly melody, intolerably sweet."

Our soul must be transformed into Christlikeness as we more fully participate in the divine nature. (2 Peter 1:4) We are to be sanctified fully in Christ—soul, and body. The Spirit must have more of us if we are to be progressively sanctified and this is a journey. This is the greatest of the journey, it is our calling and our inheritance. This is what it means to be constantly filled with the Spirit. (Ephesians 5:18)

To summarize again, we have been justified in Christ, which includes our sanctification and we look forward to our glorification in heaven. Our sanctification is judicial or positional in Christ and therefore, we can have communion with a holy God, but we are also to go on to be progressively practically sanctified in soul and body. This is our calling while on earth and out of this love relationship with Christ, we will fulfill the great calling. We are sanctified and we are being sanctified as we participate in the process. "For by one offering, He has perfected forever those who are *being sanctified*" (Hebrews 10:14).

"Outward sanctification is not enough without inward, nor inward without outward. We must have both "clean hands and a pure heart."[7] Certainly, those who become Christians will give evidence of knowing God in Christ. They will love God and love others—especially other Christians. Their basic desires will change and they will love God and His purposes. They will grow in their trust of Him and will seek to find and follow His will for their life and the church." If you truly love God, doing what you want will be doing what God wants."[8] They will grow in knowledge and grace. But to what extent—this is very important. It is not just what comes easy and just enough to get by, but his disciples will they love God with all their heart, mind, soul, and body? They will not be people who just cruise through this life and basically eternally waste it, but discipline their lives to honor God and His inheritance for us fully?

We will be held accountable for what we have done with the inheritance we have in Christ. We will be rewarded, or we will be passed over. However, let us be clear the reward is, in fact, the continuation of the quality of the love relationship we have with our Triune God in this life. It is never too late to start. It will make a difference in eternity. "If the Lord is God, follow him; but if Baal (or money, or Power, or Security) is God, follow him (1 Kings 18:21).[9] Jesus said, "For where you treasure is, there your heart will be also" (Matthew 6:21).

"Draw near to God, and he will draw near to you. Cleanse your hands, you sinners, and purify your hearts, you double-minded. Be wretched and mourn and weep. Let your laughter be turned to mourning and your joy to gloom. Humble yourselves before the Lord, and he will exalt you." (James 4:8-10).

CHAPTER 6

THE OVERVIEW OF THE PROCESS OF SPIRITUAL FORMATION

"Pray without ceasing" (1 Thessalonians 5:17) A life of Prayer

Jesus made prayer a priority. (Matthew 14:23) He not only prayed He made His life a life of prayer. We tend to think of prayer, primarily as talking to God and giving Him our requests, but prayer, as Jesus lived, it was mostly about listening to the Father. He is a great listener. Jesus said, "For I have not spoken on my own authority, but the Father who sent me has himself given me a commandment--what to say and what to speak. And I know that his commandment is eternal life. What I say, therefore, I say as the Father has told me." (John 12:49-50). He also said, "The Son can do nothing of his own accord, but only what He sees the Father doing. For whatever the Father does, the Son also does in likewise" (John 5:19). Again, He says, "I can do nothing on my own. As I hear, I judge, and my judgment is just because I seek not my own will but the will of him who sent me" (John 5:30). Yet again, "Yet even if I do judge, my judgment is true, for it is not I alone who judge, but I and the Father who sent me (John 8:16). God speaks to those who listen. Jesus lived the will of the Father and so are we to do likewise, if we are his disciples. Jesus was in total synch with the Father and so are we to be in full union with him, if we are to glorify the Father as did Jesus. Because Jesus lived a life of prayer, he was in complete union with the Father. Jesus invited us to the fulness of life and said "follow me—be my disciple."

Contemplative prayer is primarily listening to God. It means making much room for God. It is time that is fully devoted to God—not distracted or pressured by things that must be done in our day or that we want to do. In the beginning, this is especially difficult. Distractions will constantly seek to rush upon us. If we stay with prayer, we can move past this and tune our ears to hear from God. It may at times seem like nothing is happening, but God does great things in us, even when we don't realize it. Jesus was a great listener and men and women in the Bible, including the prophets and Kings, were good listeners of God. When we look at, for instance, God's beautiful creation, we at times, are in Awe. This is similar to being in Awe of God, for He is very beautiful, and as we listen to Him and direct our gaze and our heart in love to Him. Prayer is an attentive, loving gaze on Jesus.

Jesus taught much about prayer and practiced, so much that the disciples noticed he spent considerable time in prayer, they asked Him to teach them to pray. (Luke 11:1) Jesus spent forty days fasting and praying in the desert before he began his ministry. (Matthew 4:1-11) Prayer was not just tacked onto His life, he enjoyed spending time with the Father and knew he needed to depend entirely upon him and his direction. He loved to pray and made a great effort to spend time alone so He could focus Himself totally on the Father. (Matthew 14:23) The discipline of prayer can release our full-blown desire for God and His beauty. "One of the fruits of prayer is that it gives us a progressively deeper knowledge of God and ourselves."[1]

I believe the practice of praying without ceasing (1 Thessalonians 5:17) is more of an attitude of prayer. It is an attitude that is largely and primarily focused on Jesus with our heart, mind, soul, and strength. It is a way of life. However, it comes out of making prayer a huge priority in our lives. If a Christian hasn't learned the benefits of making their life a life of prayer, they are missing out on the biggest blessing in this life other than Jesus Himself—after all, prayer is about being close to our Triune God.

Many would say, "I can hardly spend five minutes in prayer, for when I set aside time to pray, all these distracting thoughts come into my head. I can barely get through the five minutes." This is not unusual. Many that begin in prayer or begin again will have this experience. This is just the first barrier to breakthrough.

Why does Satan attack us so much and try to throw all kinds of obstacles in our way of Bible reading and study and prayer? It is because it is so vital to our ongoing relationship with God and influence and ministry to others. He doesn't want us focused on or be listening or being guided by God, he wants us to wallow in the shallow end. He wants to make us vulnerable to temptations. "Lead us not into temptation." We are led into temptation when we neglect our spiritual development. Satan usually leads us down the garden path and then mounts a surprise attack. A Christian without prayer is like a fish out of water or a bird not able to fly. If we don't nourish our relationship with God, we weaken it, as is also applicable in a friendship or marriage.

. . .

Most Christians spend little time in prayer. J.C. Ryle said, "I am convinced that the vast majority of professing Christians do not pray." If this was true in Ryle's day, the early 19 century, think about what it is like today with all our possible distractions. Maybe when they first became a Christian, people were first excited about the newness and the beauty of the relationship with God and spent time in prayer, but somehow it has waned. However, there is hope, we can refresh our relationship with God and go on to new heights, never yet experienced, that will draw us ever closer to God and far outweigh the resistance from the evil one. The more and more we truly pray, the more we will want to spend time with God—however, there will be dry periods when we make room for God, even when we don't especially feel close to Him. Even in these times of aridity, we will have a sense of him, though slight. We will explore this aspect in more detail later.

CHAPTER 7

TYPES OF PRAYER

There is vocal prayer as when we say prayers out loud, like the Lord's Prayer. There may also be other read prayers said in a congregation during worship or spontaneous prayer spoken during the worship or at other times. We also may be overcome by God at times and say a vocal prayer as a way of expressing our desires and love of God. Some prefer, when they are praying by themselves, to pray in a quiet voice, so they can focus much better.

The most common private prayer is mental prayer. This is where we say our prayers or have an attitude of prayer in our minds and heart. We may express our love, trust, and loyalty to God and bring our requests to Him and seek His direction and present our lives to Him so that He, might live in and through us and let him reveal our sins and shortcomings. Some think they can do this kind of prayer while driving their car working, or walking. Yes, they can, but it is not as focused and perhaps it doesn't show much respect if this is the only prayer that we practice. How do you feel when you are talking to someone and they are constantly looking at their phone? God deserves our full attention and our full devotion. It is unlikely we are going to hear Him if we are constantly occupied with other factors. People often get busy to avoid spending time with God, for it is a fearful thing at times to come before God with our human nature, for God not only reveals Himself but ourselves.

The most beautiful type of prayer is contemplative prayer. "In the first kind of prayer, one thinks upon God; in the other, one beholds Him. The second is a purer practice."[1] As Madame Guyon said, it is a prayer "of the heart." "Contemplation leads to, or rather is an experience of transcendence—that is, of forgetfulness of self and everyone and everything, else except the contemplative object."[2]

Again, we are all familiar with contemplating the beauty of nature, especially in a very picturesque scene. Sometimes this also occurs when we think theologically. We not only appreciate the beauty, but we encounter it and somehow become a part of it. It is an experience of the heart as well as the mind. In contemplative prayer, we enter more fully into God and are refreshed and replenished in His beauty and goodness. We truly enjoy God. We truly love Him in this exercise for God is love and we need first to experience God in love if we are truly to know love. (1 John 4:10-12; 1 John 4:8) Those you love you want to spend time with.

We often spend a lot of time talking to God out loud or in our minds, but we don't spend a lot of time listening. Elijah went up to the mountain as God instructed and there was a strong wind, an earthquake, and a fire, but God was in any of them. God spoke in "a still small voice" (1 Kings 19:12). Often, we look for God in the spectacular, but God is gently speaking to our hearts and mind. It, however, takes great focus, devotion, and dedication to hear Him. That is because evil is still in our world and we are still influenced by the effects of the fallen nature that has not been yet restored to complete health, in practice, like in heaven, and Satan is against us advancing in our relationship with God in prayer. And God does not force himself on the unwilling.

Contemplative prayer is not learned overnight. It comes out of perseverance in prayer and it is also a gift given by God Himself. "Then He spoke a parable to them, that men always ought to pray and not lose heart' (|Luke 18:1). This is not an easy road, maybe that is why there are few on it. The spiritual battle will be great, but the drawing of the Lord is much greater.

John of the Cross said, "This contemplation is an outpouring of God into the soul, a divine, loving knowledge that is general, without images or concepts, obscure and hidden from the one who receives it, a knowledge that both purifies and illumines... An attitude of personal and complete receptivity before God who is communicating Himself in His personal infinitude."[3]

It is only in listening that we are transformed in Christ. We must agree with God about all our sins and shortcoming and turn to Him in repentance and acceptance of His grace and faith to make us new in practice. Only He can truly transform us within. By our will, we can reform ourselves, but in Christ, we can be transformed. Satan comes to destroy us and attack our personhood and God the Holy Spirit comes to release us to be all we are called to be in Christ. We can only truly learn prayer by praying, yet it is good to know some factors that others have learned through the centuries about the process of spiritual formation that God commonly uses.

CHAPTER 8

REACHING THE HEIGHTS

"The wind blows where it wishes, and you hear its sound, but you do not know where it comes from or where it goes. So, it is with everyone who is born of the Spirit" (John 3:8).

There have been those who have gone before us, many of them much more dedicated than us. The early desert Fathers in the third and fourth centuries lived remarkable lives of prayer in solitude in the desert.[1] This includes the life of Antony written by the Theologian Athanasius.[2] They went out to the desert primarily because of the worldliness of society and the church. What they learned in spending very dedicated time with the Lord they passed on to others. There have been many in the Spiritual Theology field that has passed on the knowledge, skills, experience, and practice done with 2000 years of church history. We would be foolish to not glean from them, a precious treasure in the Kingdom of God.

. . .

It is wise to be aware of the pitfalls, discouragements, deceptions, and frustrations of the journey if we are not going to turn back, camp out, or live a bitter and unproductive life. If we are going to train cattle cutting horses it would be good to learn from others. This will avoid developing habits hard to break in the horse and a great deal of discouragement and frustration. The same applies to the spiritual formation journey. "Be not like the horse or the mule, without understanding, which must be curbed with a bit and bridle, or it will not stay near you" (Psalm 32:9).

John Calvin said, "The human heart is a factory of idols." How true! Spiritual formation deals with all the idols of the heart. David Hubbard said in the Preachers Commentary on Proverbs, "No pain and no gain is not only the rule of physical fitness, it applies equally to moral and spiritual development." Those committed to a life of ease and comfort over God will never take this road. "Prayer makes us enter more and more deeply into God's light, and like a ray of sunlight coming into a dark room and revealing the tiniest speck of dust floating in the air, that lays bare our imperfections and sin."[3] However, it is worth it. Those fully on this journey want nothing that corrupts us and our world and nothing that hinders our relationship with God and certainly not anything that does not Glorify God and his goodness.

What is the mark that we are to hit? It is God and full union with him. No longer in primary union with sin, self, and the world, but with someone much greater and who is the essence of everything that is good and beautiful. It is said that Satan was once one of the most beautiful angels in heaven before his fall into sin. (Ezekiel 28:17) However, his beauty is nothing compared to God. As King David said in the Psalms, "One thing I have asked of the Lord, that I will seek after: that I may dwell in the house of the Lord all the days of my life, to gaze on the beauty of the Lord and to inquire in his temple" (Psalm 27:4).

. . .

God covered his beauty in Jesus Christ, so that we would not just desire him for his beauty, but that we sincerely love him for his true self. The Godhead was veiled in Jesus Christ. The scripture prophecy about Jesus when the prophet Isaiah says, "For he grew up before him like a young plant, and like a root out of the dry ground; he had no form or majesty that we should look at him, and no beauty that we should desire him" (Isaiah 53:2).

We can seek God primarily for what he does for us or for what we can get from him. Just like this is not a fine recipe for friendship in this world, so it is not with God. We must remember he is the goal, not primarily the results or blessings that come from the goal." Therefore, as you enjoy the process of ongoing conversion, never take your eyes off the ultimate end: God Himself. Spiritual fulfillment, delights, virtues, experiences, consolations, etc., are not the ultimate end. God and God alone is the ultimate end. If you remember that, you will keep moving and be constantly moving toward God in His fullness."[4] As Saint John of the Cross said, "He is always looking at you; can you not turn the eyes of your soul to look at Him?[5]

CHAPTER 9

STAGES ALONG THE WAY

"**B**lessed are the pure in heart, for they shall see God" (Matthew 5:8)

Do we want to see God as he is or as we have conceived him to be or worse yet, made him be? To see God takes a great desire, strength of purpose, and great dedication. Why is it so hard? It is because at the root of our being, without Christ, we are enormously corrupted by sin and darkness. (Jeremiah 17:9) There are many misconceptions to overcome, much of sinful pride to lay aside, and much of the old self to make room for God—much room for he is God. As John Paul Thomas has said, "God cannot be "solved."[1] We cannot put God in a box and carry him around with us. God's magnitude is beyond our comprehension, but we can seek to comprehend him as much as possible in knowledge, wisdom, experience, and practice. We have eternity to learn of his vastness.

Throughout the centuries, according to largely agreed upon Spiritual Theology, there are three stages that a person goes through in coming into full union with God. The first is the purgative way, the second is the illuminative way and the third is the unitive way.[2] In the big picture, one stage leads to another, but they often overlap and they are all part of the overall journey.

The Purgative Way

From my studies, the best Spiritual directors that explain the process of spiritual formation is Saint John of the Cross (1542-1591) and Saint Theresa of Avila (1515 -1582). They are identified with what is now called Carmelite Spirituality. They tend to lay a clear but in-depth road map for the process that is involved in the plan God has for our life to experience the fullness that is in Christ. (Ephesians 3:19) It is helpful to learn from others who had gone before us and experienced full union with God, which was evidenced in their lives. This process was first explained by the writer called Dionysius in his writing of the *Divine Names* and *The Mystical Theology*. This could go back to the first, second, or third century.[3] There is some debate on the date and the author of the writing. However, it was early and beneficial.

The name Carmelite is derived from the ministry of Elijah and his experiences with God at Mount Carmel. There Elijah took on the 450 false prophets of Baal and 400 false prophets of Asherah and displayed the glory and power of the Lord. (1 Kings 18:19) In a sense, the process of spiritual formation is dealing with many idols that come in our way to intimacy with God, especially the idol of self. Saint John of the Cross was a spiritual director to Theresa of Avila, but they assisted one another and worked together in reforming the monasteries in the Carmelite order, primarily in Spain during the fifteenth century.

We must be purified in the heart if we are going to be able to see God very clearly and experience him more fully. We all must deal with a distorted view of God, theologically and spiritually, because of sin and the darkness that sin brings into our life and the world. As mentioned before, every Christian has a new heart, but not every Christian is experiencing the fullness of this new heart. There is a process that must be actualized. If it is not, we will still be contaminated, some more than others. When this occurs, we are an easy target of the evil one. This process goes beyond the basics of dealing with sin on the outside. Remember that St. John of the Cross is writing to committed followers of Jesus Christ who have denied themselves to follow Christ. Spiritual formation goes beyond the basics of discipleship, but it is the foundation of discipleship.

God said to his people Israel, "These people draw near with their mouth and honor me with their lips, while their hearts are far from me" (Isaiah 29:13). People can be going through the motions of worshipping God and serving Him, but their root desires are not with God but with the world, the flesh, and the devil. Jesus said, "For out of the heart come evil thoughts, murder, adultery, sexual immorality, theft, false witness, slander. These are what defile a person" (Matthew 15:19). This being the case, how earnestly should we deal with issues of the heart. God sees our heart and sees it in its corruption or purity. We don't want to be like the Pharisees and just clean up the outside of the cup and the inside be full of dirt. (Matthew 23:25)

This issue of full union with God has as its foundation freedom. Only when we are free as possible from the corruptions of sin are we truly free. Freedom is the heart cry of democracy and also of man in this world. God wants us to fully experience freedom because, in this freedom, we will truly experience fullness and fulfillment. Why would we pursue pride which only brings us into bondage and destruction, like the devil? Yet, many think this is the road to freedom. Consider that ultimate ruin of the evil one. "Chose your stance—whether pride or humility—and you have chosen the companion who will either drag you into shame or lead you into wisdom"[4] As Saint John of the Cross proposes, "When God's will and the souls are in conformity so that nothing in the one is repugnant to the other and the soul is completely rid of selfishness, rests transformed in God through love."[5]

Only God can give us a new heart when we are born again and only Christ can cleanse our hearts as we co-operate with Him and cultivate a receptivity, which occurs when we practice a life of prayer. "To ignore our need for purification is the worst kind of personal self-deception."[6] We certainly don't want to be like the false prophets in Jeremiah's day, which Jeremiah said, "They have also healed the hurt of My people slightly" (Jeremiah 6:14). "It is specifically the hearts of his people that God calls in conversion.... The heart is the place in which God recreates us in his own image and likeness, transforming and purging us: "Yahweh, your God, will circumcise your heart... until you love him with all your heart (Dt.30:6) ...Create in me, O God, a cleansed heart. Renew a steadfast spirit within me. (Ps 51:10)"[7]

"Satan has no need to tempt those who tempt themselves and are continually dragged down by worldly affairs. And know this too: the prizes and crowns are given to those who are tested by temptation—not to those who care nothing about God, to the worldly who lie on their backs and snore."[8] Do not deal with the process of spiritual growth, discipleship, and spiritual formation and you will be being set up for harassment and the road to foolishness. "The devil's favorite and more effective ploy is to deceive people 'under the guise of good rather than evil."[9] John Bunyan, in his book, *The Pilgrims Progress*, mentions many snares that Satan uses to try and divert us. As the apostle, Peter states, "Be soberminded; be watchful. Your adversary the devil prowls around like a roaring lion, seeking someone to devour" (1 Peter 5:8). Spiritual formation in Christ deals with the root issues. These are the front lines of defense and offense against sin and the evil one.

Purgation can be a painful process. Fortunately, it is mixed in with consolations of the Lord. His consolations are far more than our purgations, though, at times, they can be intense. It may seem like we are losing ourselves. What is actually happening is that we are losing our old self, the old man as the Bible states, and fully entering into the new man in Christ. (Ephesians 4:22) Along these lines, Jesus said, "Whoever seeks to save his life will *lose it*, and whoever *loses his life* will preserve it" (Luke 17:33). However, some grief may be involved in giving up our old ways and matters of the heart. "To obtain all that was just mentioned, the soul must be completely annihilated in its former and lower self. This will be painful because the soul will be radically and completely transformed. Change can hurt."[10] "I have been crucified with Christ. It is no longer I that live but Christ, but Christ who lives in me" (Galatians 2:20) We may have great attachments to this coping mechanism we have used because we think that they benefit us more than entering fully into Christ in practice and experience. They only hold us back from the fullness that God has planned for us. "The painful purgation of the sensual human nature (the appetites, passions, desires) will be helped by prayer, mortification and intentional acts of virtue."[11]

A beginner is one who has dealt and is dealing with outward sin and is practicing a life of virtue and prayer. Going forward, we must stay in prayer as God reveals himself experientially to us and reveals ourselves, as we are grounded in the assurance of God's love for us. When we know, we are loved and are assured of his love, we can face the corruption within. To be strengthened in this, we only need to be reminded of the cross and the magnitude of God's humility and love. We confess our sin as it is revealed— every form of pride and so forth. We don't deal with this only outwardly but inwardly. However, this threatens Satan, so be prepared for a battle. Practice prayer even when it is arid and when you sense you are under attack, eventually, there will be breakthroughs and it will be worth it all. Far more than we can imagine. (Ephesians 3:20)

In a sense, purgation is a continuing process, but at some point, we become more proficient in prayer. As we progress in prayer and spiritual formation, we will start to experience some form of contemplation in prayer. A consolation for the Lord. A sense of heaven here on earth. It can motivate us to keep pressing in.

We go from beginner to proficient when we have initially been purged in our senses according to St. John of the Cross and we enter the illuminative stage of spiritual formation. John of the Cross says we will also go through a dark night of the senses and of the spirit as we progress and we will consider it more fully a little later.

The Illuminative Way

The illuminative way is not just understanding scripture but seeing God more clearly in our hearts and experiencing his grace more fully. St. John of the Cross calls the people at the illuminative stage proficient. However, don't be obsessed with analyzing at what stage you are at, or you will only become self-centered. Let God determine where you are at and lead you. We don't control the process God does. When driving a car, "We don't paste the map on the windshield and contemplate it as we travel; we would surely crash. But it is a very good idea to have the map beside us on the seat for consultation when we are in doubt."[12]

There are two stages of purification that St. John of the Cross teaches that a person must go through to become proficient. The first stage is the purification of the senses. There is the co-operative purification of the senses and the passive purification of the senses. The senses have to do with our desires, our ambitions, and our basic human appetites. As mentioned, these are corrupted by sin and must be purified by the Holy Spirit and re-ordered to health in Christ, and this occurs as we examine our hearts with the assistance of the Holy Spirit and repent of the sin involved or contaminating our senses and spirit. In like manner, Socrates said, "The unexamined life is not worth living."

Our senses are our appetites, desires, and will. This is when the purification process gets really serious. These are not to be done away with but to be re-ordered. They must be purified and orientated by God and to God to experience God's way, which is love.

The root sins have to do with pride in its multiple forms and the other of the seven deadly sins. These are at the root of sins. The root must be dealt with if the tree is going to be healthy. Too often, we are only dealing with the symptoms rather than the root.

Purgation is a painful process, that is perhaps why few are on this road. "It's as if, in the cocoon, the soul is watching its old self be destroyed. Though its subsequent emergence is ultimately glorious, there is still a pain associated with the death of the old self."[13] Many would prefer to live the Christian life, just by the strength of their own will. The will is important, but grace is far more important to be living in the fulness that God plans for us. God's grace can empower the will. Purification of the will is a very deep manner. That is why there is a passive purgation of the senses. It is a deep work of God; it is often mysterious as we stay before him in prayer. God touches us deeper down than we can ever fully understand, but we can experience the effects in our life. "The wind blows where it wills." (John 3:8). *The word passive for Saint John of the Cross, "does not mean that we lack a vital role, but that God is the principal-agent and we respond as receivers."*[14]

We will have to face many of the lies we have based our life on and our approach to life. I guess, in a way, it is similar to therapeutic counseling, but with a counselor that is all-wise and that can be completely trusted and that does not only expose the issues but heals by his grace the root of the problem as we grow in spiritual maturity. He is the "wonderful counselor" (Isaiah 9:6). Along these lines, John Paul Thomas says, "If "purgation" sounds painful, difficult and depressing, that is because you have allowed yourself to be deceived by the world, the flesh, the evil one, and your own misguided will. Do you want the truth, or do you prefer to live in a lie?" It may be hard from the human side, but powerful from the divine. It is the way of life. Jesus said, "Come to me, all who labor and are heavy laden, and I will give you rest. Take my yoke upon you, and learn from me, for I am gentle and lowly in heart, and you will find rest for your souls. For my yoke is easy, and my burden is light" (Matthew 11:28-30). If we try to do it only in our strength, it will be a burden, but in the Lord, it is easy. It is not easy if done in our own strength and can be totally frustrating. However, pride makes us want to walk in our strength. It is easy because God is all-powerful and can transform us and he brings with himself fulfillment.

St. John wrote these primary writings—The Spiritual Canticle, The Ascent of Mount Carmel, The Living Flame, and The Dark Night. "The ascent of the mountain, even more than the Exodus, became the favorite image of the spiritual life. By the time of St. Gregory of Nyssa (died AD 394), it was already part of the tradition in Christian spirituality."[15] In the Life of Moses, St. Gregory of Nyssa says, "The knowledge of God is a mountain steep indeed and difficult to climb—the majority of people scarcely reach its base.[16]

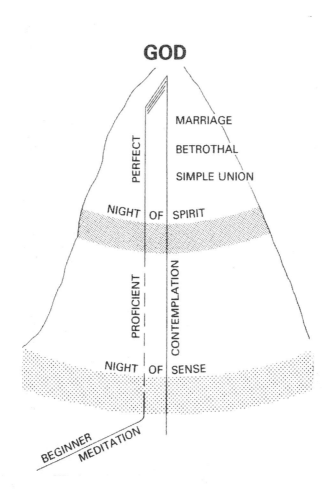

This illustration lays out the normal general plan that God takes people through in spiritual formation as learned through the ages and clarified by St. John of the Cross.[17] He lays out two stages of purification that we go through, as we proceed up the mountain to full union with God. In the Purgation stage, there is the purification of the senses, and included in this stage, we must pass through a dark night of the senses. In this stage, there is the active part of the purification in which we largely co-operate with God, and then there, is what he calls the passive part of the purification of the senses in which God more largely primarily takes does the work. Later in the illuminative stage, there is the purification of the spirit, the active and the passive parts. Each has a dark night that you must pass through to get higher up the mountain. We must be purified fully to be in a very close relationship with God. (James 4:7-8) Going through the dark knight requires faith and builds up faith. It is faith-centered in the love of God.

Going through the dark night really refines our faith. We are purified of wanting God only for experiences of him or blessings from him. We learn to love him entirely for himself. "The mark of a good prayer life is not abundant consolations, but growth in virtues."[18]At times, it is dark because often there is a sense of aridity. We may not feel close to the Lord, but we know he is working. We truly walk by faith and not by sight. We yearn even more for God, during this time. Our yearning helps to purify our hearts. Trust the Lord through this dark night and continue to spend quality time dedicated to the Lord, especially in prayer. The dark night is times of aridity. "Many people enter the night—or nights, since there are several—but very few persevere until the end of the journey."[19]

Dryness in prayer might be because the beginner has not learned to pray. It also may be because of negligence or disordered attachments or willful sin in our lives. It may also be because of the spiritual process that God is taking us through. We need to be discerning. As Saint John of the Cross said, "It is dark not because the Lord is absent but because he is too present—to close, that is, to us sinners. Our eyes cannot stand his light. We are blinded by his brightness."[20]As Thomas H. Green states, "So it is that we return now to the experience of darkness and dryness which I am convinced is the normal lot of those who are faithful to their life of prayer. Although we cannot fully understand this experience until we are able to see it whole from the other side of the grave, I think it should be possible now to understand better the mysterious process which leads from dryness to floating."[21]

Bernard of Clairvaux states that there are four stages in our journey in loving God. The first stage is When man loves himself for his own sake. The second stage is when man loves God for his own good. The third stage is when man loves God for God's sake and the fourth stage is when man loves himself for the sake of God.[22] This is much deeper than it seems. The fourth stage goes even beyond loving God for Himself and we choose to entirely find our worth and identity in Christ and love ourselves only or primarily for God's sake. Our old self is small and God then is large in our lives.

Yes. There is a cooperative part that is involved in purgation and a passive part. Just a word to those who are Theologians, although we are all, in a sense, all Theologians. We live our life based on our Theology. That is scary because how we live shows what we truly believe about God. (Proverbs 23:7) To address this matter is an issue of enormous theological investigation and yet it is going to be addressed initially in one paragraph. It is about God's Sovereignty and Human Responsibility, which are both taught in the Bible. Certainly, God's Sovereignty is above even human responsibility, but both must be held in balance.[23] We may not understand how they both come together, but we know enough to hold them together as friends. There is a sense in which monergism and syncretism are involved in our salvation and in Christian growth. "C. H. Spurgeon was once asked if he could reconcile these two truths to each other. "I wouldn't try," he replied; "I never reconcile friends." Friends? —yes, friends. This is the point that we have to grasp. In the Bible, divine sovereignty and human responsibility are not enemies. They are not uneasy neighbors; they are not in an endless state of cold war with each other. They are friends, and they work together."[24]

To move into the illuminated way does not only mean that we are only illuminated about scripture, although this is important and does occur, it means we are illuminated about God—we see or experience or love God more fully. In the book, *A Treatise on Prayer and Mediation,* Saint Teresa of Avila said, "In prayer, the soul is purified from sin, charity is nurtured, faith takes root, hope is strengthened, the spirit gladdened. In prayer, the soul melts in tenderness, the heart is purified, the truth reveals itself, the temptation is overcome, and sadness is put to flight. In prayer, the senses renewed, lukewarmness vanishes, failing virtue is reinvigorated, the rust of vices is scoured away; and in this exchange, there come forth the living sparks, blazing desires of heaven, in which the flame of divine love burns."[25]

As we step into the illuminative way, it is a new kind of freedom and intimacy with God. "As you grow in your Christian life, God will bring you through the active and passive purgation of your senses and draw you into the life of a proficient, which is the Illuminative Way. This could be termed your second conversion."[26] Some Christians find their way here without understanding all of the processes. They are just progressing with the Lord and have quality time set aside for prayer. However, many get derailed and think God has abandoned them and either give up or settle for mediocracy. Some just become better actors and learn better to control their outward behavior and others and manipulate their world.

The Unitive Way

The third part of the journey is the purification of the spirit, going through this stage will lead us to the highest stage, the unitive way. As the scriptures state, "Since we have these promises, beloved, let us cleanse ourselves from every defilement of body *and spirit,* bringing holiness to completion in fear of God" (2

Corinthians 7:1). (See also 2 Thessalonians 5:23) Again, there is a cooperative part of the cleansing of our spirit and a passive part. This process cleanses our spirit from the deception, distortions, and misrepresentation of the evil one, and purifies the love we hold for God and others. We also become more competent at the discernment of spirits. (1 Corinthians 12:10) In the process, our faith is also built up by knowing God more fully and experientially, and in actuality. As Job says after going through some major trials, "I had heard of you by the hearing of the ear, but now my eyes see you" (Job 42:5). The process is quite mysterious, but it deals with the very essence of what is distorted attachments and perceptions. It clears the glass so we can see clearly and trust God more perfectly and walk-in sync with him more consistently. "In prayer, there is a mystery that absolutely surpasses our understanding."[27]

The third stage of the overall process of spiritual formation is the Unitive way. Not many find this way. "Saint John tells us that very few people in this life actually attain divine union."[28] Not many desire God enough and put enough effort into experiencing God in this way. Not many are diligent enough to keep their heart. (Proverbs 4:23) As Jacques Phillippe has said along these lines, "Truly, thou are a God who hidest thyself, O God of Israel, the Savior" (Isaiah 45:15). The only way to bring him out of his hiding place is by searching for him in love. Faith and love "break his cover: whereas all other means are useless. God cannot be found or possessed except by faith and love because he does not want to be united to us in any other way except a loving encounter."[29] Many of the saints refer to the Song of Songs as a passionate yearning and search in love for God.

We tend to seek God for the wrong reasons, and if we do so, we will not find him. We must be purified to find the unitive way, which is a very close intimacy with God in heart, mind, will, and strength. To love him in this way is the calling of all who are Christian. (Ephesians 4:1) Why do so few seek him in this way? So easy to waste time in our society and any time throughout history.

What will it be like to stand before Jesus and realize that we have wasted much of our life? (Matthew 25:23) We may have invested wisely financially in this life, but what about in eternity? What have we invested in eternity? "The one who receives a prophet because he is a prophet will receive a prophet's reward, and the one who receives a righteous person because he is a righteous person will receive a righteous person's reward. And whoever gives one of these little ones even a cup of cold water because he is a disciple, truly, I say to you, he will by no means lose his reward" (Matthew 10:41-42). We can use our resources to primarily advance God's kingdom or our own. The scripture shows us again and again that God is very interested in the state of our heart, perhaps more than our actions. "In sacrifice and offering, you have not delighted, but you have given me an open ear. Burnt offering and sin offering you have not required. Then I said, "Behold, I have come; in the scroll of the book, it is written of me; I delight to do your will, O my God; your law is within my heart" (Psalm 40:6-8).

In the Old Testament and the worship of God, God was very interested in being cleansed to come to worship him. The outward cleanings were pointing to an inward cleansing that was the essence of what God desired for us. The priests and the people had to practice many aspects of cleaning and it was very important to be clean to come into the temple or place of worship. The temple was set up with an outer court, the Holy place, and then a thick curtain that separated the Holy of Holies. Only the priest would enter the Holy of Holies once a year to see if the sacrifices of the people were accepted by God. Only after cleansing would the priest enter the holy of holies and that with a rope tied to his ankle. If the sacrifices were not accepted by God for the people, the priest would die and he would need to be dragged by the rope. When Christ died on the cross, the curtain separating the holy of holies was torn in two. Now those who receive Christ can enter the holy of holies; *God wants us now to primarily live there while on earth*, to live in this state. Judicially or positionally in Christ, we can now enter, but experientially and practically, we may not

73

be fully living in this state. We may be living in the outer courts of the temple area. To be living in the holy of holies also means that we are also living in a state of prayer. Our love for God is great and he has incorporated Himself fully into our life. (Galatians 2:20) This is not like being a casual tourist touring the temple, but for those who are truly comfortable in the Holy of Holies and enjoy fully the depths of the riches in Christ. (Ephesians 3:18) These people are truly experiencing and enjoying God to his full extent and are in full union with Him. This is what it means, in essence, to glorify God and enjoy Him.

The Puritans and the saints of old also speak of the Unitive way as being a spiritual marriage and would see a book like the Song of Solomon as an analogy of our love relationship to our Triune God.[30] Some of the saints also call it experiencing the beatific vision of God. The eastern Orthodox form of spirituality refers to the unitive way as the hypostatic union, where the divine and human become one individual. This, I believe, is not what Saint John of the Cross talks about. We become one in a union, but we are still distinct—two becoming one in heart, mind strength, and will. This is when saints experience God in a great deal of his beauty. They truly see God completely with their heart in his fulness. This is similar to how Moses saw God's glory and how Peter, James, and John experienced Christ in the transfiguration. (Exodus 33; Matthew 17:1-6)

Saint Teresa of Avila explains the contemplative prayer and the growth toward the unitive way by the analogy of obtaining water. Vocal prayer is like going to the river and carrying back water back in a bucket. Discursive prayer is largely a meditation on God and this is pictured as when we go to pump water from a well and carry the water in a bucket. Unfortunately, this is the place most Christians end up. Then there is effective mediation. This is when we are beginning to enter contemplative prayer. It is when we truly are more fully experiencing God in our state of being and in prayer. At this point in the analogy, the person is sitting beside the creek or river and the water is coming to them. It is at this point that people will experience the night of aridity, where God may withdraw, and more earnestly is our desire for him purified. Then the most beautiful stage of prayer is where the water is raining down upon us and this is contemplative prayer. Saint Theresa also says, "When a soul stays in one state, I don't consider it safe." In other words, if we don't progress in our prayer life, we are open to self-deception and deception by the evil one.

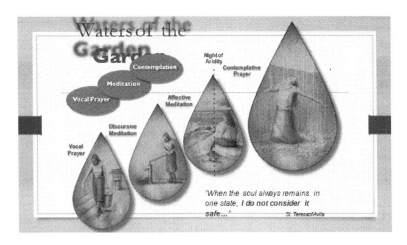

In Saint Theresa of Avila's books, especially *The Interior Castle*, she explains in another way the process of spiritual formation from a vision given to her by the Lord.[31] The analogy is that of a castle with many rooms or mansions, as she calls them. In each room, we advance towards spiritual marriage, the beatific vision, or full union with God. One room leads to the next. There are no shortcuts. In the first room, purgative asceticism progress is the work of man aided by God. When we progress at the beginning of contemplative prayer to the heights, we are active and diligent, but progress is primarily the work of God. In the stage of contemplative prayer, we progress from what she calls the prayer of quiet a divine attentiveness (to the prayer of union, to conforming union and then to transforming union as we fully enter the unitive way.)

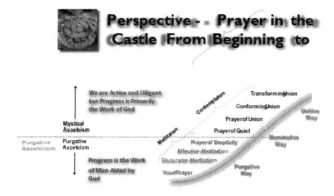

Perspective - Prayer in the Castle From Beginning to

As Martin Luther said, "God becomes man that dehumanized men might become true men." This part of the result of finding the unitive way. We become our true selves. Ourselves in God's image that we were created to be. Until we find this way, we are truly lost. Man lives a divided life, divided from self, others, and primarily God. In Christ, we come back to full sanity. Karen Horney, the psychologist, said the man has a despised self and an ideal self. Our ideal self may be an illusion of ourselves, but mankind prefers to hold this illusion rather than give up in despair. However, this does not lead to being self-aware and fully alive. Horney states the best way to live in this broken world is to live in your real self. Jesus lets us live in our true selves. "John of the Cross held firmly the conviction that in order to reach one's potential as a human being, one needed to strive to encounter intimacy with God, a striving that became a primary focus of his mentoring relationships. He was especially concerned with teaching souls, "the dynamics of growth in union with God."[32] However, not everyone is a beginner, as St. John of the Cross understands them to be and is not ready for spiritual direction. They must be practicing the basics of scripture reading and prayer before beginning spiritual direction. They must have a consistent prayer life. However, St. Bernard of Clairvaux said, "Anyone who takes himself for his own spiritual director is a disciple of a fool." We need each other and this is the way God planned it. We walk together to the glory of God. Spiritual direction from those who are on the path can assist them in understanding how God is working in our lives and come in union with God and be assisted in understanding how God is leading. It is primarily as a guide in the life of prayer or connecting and being in sync with God.

Counseling is very distinct from spiritual direction. Psychology is focused on understanding what influences us and spiritual direction is primarily interested in how God is influencing us. Some need counseling to assist them in their spiritual development, some need both and some just need spiritual direction. Spiritual direction is about the quality of our relationship with God and our prayer life. This is some overlap in psychology and spiritual formation, but the tendency is to make spiritual direction into counseling rather than to be focused on God. Our focus in counseling is on self and in spiritual direction, it is on God. Sometimes a spiritual director will refer the one being directed to a counselor to deal with psychological issues. Our spiritual formation will affect us psychologically, but psychology does not necessarily affect our spirituality if the ultimate focus is still on ourselves. In psychology, we learn what affects us and understand how we can better react to our world and live-in relationship with others. In the spiritual direction, we learn to do the will of God and enjoy him in his fullness. It assists us primarily in our prayer life in sensing God's direction and in Spiritual formation.

C.S. Lewis, in his book, *The Weight of Glory*, said, "We are half-hearted creatures fooling about with drink, sex and ambition when infinite joy is offered us, like an ignorant child who wants to on making pie in a slum because he cannot imagine what is meant by the offer of a holiday at sea. We are far too easily pleased."[33]

There is no greater contentment than fulness in Christ and the life of prayer in Christ and finding the unitive way. A lot of Christians are not experiencing this because they are not totally invested in Christ. Even Bruce Demarest, who has written many Theological books, testifies in his book *Soul Guide*, that even with his great theological knowledge and writings and his life as a professor, something was missing. He wasn't experiencing this fullness. His life was going well, but something was not as full as he knew Jesus had stated in scripture. He is a professor at Denver Seminary. He went to a seminar at a church on spiritual formation and later spent time at the Pecos Benedictine Abbey, learning spiritual formation and spiritual direction. He began experiencing more of the fullness of Christ and wrote many good books, and helped expand the spiritual formation ministry at Denver Seminary.[34] Saint Thomas Aquinas, the great Catholic Theologian who wrote many Theological and philosophical works and was considered a spiritual and theological genius by many, said later in life when he experienced the Lord in a very powerfully way, "I can write no more, I have seen things that make my writings like straw."

We are often defiant with God. We know what pleases him, but we make a game out of trying to get our way. We think it is a small thing and we think that God is surely okay with it and God certainly has a sense of humor. We are so caught up in disordered self-love that we do not conform or are not responsive to the will of God. We still think our way is better or that God can put up with it. "If obedience is preventative medicine for the soul aiming to please God, then humility is a sign that we are becoming well.... By the sheer fact that we are submissive, we block the relentless tactics of our second enemy, (the devil) who hates[35] humility in any form." Truly God's ways are not our ways. "For as the heavens are higher than the earth, so are my ways higher than your ways and my thoughts than your thoughts" (Isaiah 55:9).

In the Unitive way, our heart, mind, soul, and strength are in unison with God. Our will is in complete sync with God. The will completely or largely trusts God, the whole person puts its trust in God and his goodness and desires above all things and in all matters, even in the smallest of matters, to please him over self and to do what is His will, even though at some times it is very hard. Consider Jesus praying in the garden of Gethsemane before going to the cross. The highest good is doing the will of God in love and with love, as did Jesus. (Luke 9:23)

The Puritan William Law said, "Why am I not as holy as the early Christians? The answer must be that I do not wholly want to be." Lord, enlarge my heart and my desires for you and your will.

CHAPTER 10

ATTACHMENTS

John of the Cross talks a lot about the importance of dealing with the issue of attachments. We can have attachments that come before Christ or get in the way of our relationship to Christ—that is the reason we don't experience the fulness that God intends for us.

We must examine our lives and forgive all those people who have hurt us in the past. It is helpful in our memory to forgive all the specific times we have been harmed by specific people. Unforgiveness is a huge attachment that must be forsaken if we are going to walk close to God. "Let all bitterness and wrath and anger and clamor and slander be put away from you, along with all malice. Be kind to one another, tender-hearted, forgiving one another, as God in Christ forgave you" (Ephesians 4:31-32). If we don't forgive, we will have these attributes: bitterness, wrath, clamor, slander, and malice. We need to let the Holy Spirit examine our past hurts and, in His power, forgive. No one in their own strength forgives, but in God's strength, it happens. Love involves a lot of forgiveness. We also may need to make amends if we have injured others.

Notice how important forgiveness is in scripture. Apostle Paul says to the church at Corinth, "Anyone whom you forgive, I also forgive. Indeed, what I have forgiven, if I have forgiven anything, has been for your sake in the presence of Christ, so that we would not be outwitted by Satan, for we are not ignorant of his designs" (2 Corinthians 2:10-11). Satan wants to trip us up and hinder us by unforgiveness. Jesus says after he shared with the disciples the Lord's prayer, "But if you do not forgive others their trespasses neither will your Father forgive your trespasses" (Matthew 7:15). This sounds really serious and so it is. Unforgiveness will hinder our relationship with God. It is an attachment that will hinder the closeness we have with the Triune God.

If we are going for a hike, we wouldn't try packing a full-sized fridge on our back to hike up the hill, otherwise, we would not make much progress up the hill. Once I went backpacking, but I overpacked. I didn't weigh the backpack, but I think it was about 60 lbs., which is ridiculous. It got lighter when we went along because we ate some of the food, but I didn't want to throw any of my precious items away or litter. This made the trip very hard and somewhat torturous. On the next backpacking trip, I packed only what was absolutely essential. Many of us have attachments that hinder us from spiritually climbing Mount Carmel or any mountain of great height. If you are a rock climber, you really learn, I imagine, to pack lightly. If we are going to be spiritual climbers up the mountain, we must learn to have no attachments if we want to reach the summit.

We can have attachments that in themselves can be good things, but because they are first in heart or mind above God, they can be, in fact, be idols. If they get in the way of our close relationship to God, then they must be forsaken or laid aside, perhaps to be picked up again if they are good, when these attachments have been re-ordered. Jesus made a remarkable statement when He said, "If anyone comes to me and does not hate his father and mother and wife and children, brothers and sisters, yes, and his own life also, he cannot be My disciple. And whoever does not bear his cross and come after Me cannot be My disciple" (Luke 14:26-27). The word for hate means to love less than. Jesus will accept no place other than as God. The God, who is good and just, who can be trusted and who is all-powerful, who is the source of all goodness and love. We must also love the cross of self-denial like Jesus did. Our self-love must also not be an attachment above God and loyalty and honor to him, even to the point of death, which the early disciples experienced, all being martyred except for John, who lived to elderly age. If Jesus picked up the cross, being God in the flesh, should we not also? "Perfect union with God together with disordered attachment to creatures is an impossibility."[1]

Sometimes, we are attached to actions because they make us feel good. We may help not primarily because we love the other, but because it makes us feel good about ourselves. Sometimes the way we help people hurts those people even though it makes us feel good about ourselves. Parents also can form co-dependent relationships with their children, even though it makes the parents feel good that the children are dependent on them and grateful to them. If we constantly give children what they think they want, we create spoiled and entitled children. We hurt our children and they only learn to manipulate their world. Parents must see the bigger picture. God sees the bigger picture in His wisdom and foreknowledge and He knows what is good for us and others.

Often psychologically, we are attached to destructive patterns of behavior and perspective because we get something out of it. This also occurs in the spiritual realm. Of course, the spiritual realm does often affect the psychological realm. Our wholeness comes out of the spiritual, but there is a great interchange from one to the other, that can be complicated to learn and communicate to others. Besides that, this is more than what is the primary focus of this book. I, however, believe the best focus is on the spiritual. The spiritual will help in the process of psychological healing.

To love our family less than God does not mean we are not wise and loving and patient with them as they grow in understanding and in their relationship with the Lord, but it does mean truly to have God as our first love in our heart and mind. (Revelation 2:4) Our passion must be first truly for the Lord if He is to be truly Lord and if we are to truly love. God knows all our motives and desires and they can only come to wholeness and fullness by a transformation in Christ and so fulfill our calling in Christ. (Ephesians 4:1) Our passion for God and with God will inspire our family and others.

People who are committed to drugs or alcohol as an addiction know that these drugs affect the course of their life and their relationships with others. To have a better life, they will need to give up these attachments. Only then will this obstacle be removed from the obstruction it is to them. So, there are many ways of thinking and feeling or being at the core of who we are that are obstructing our relationship with God and the fullness of life he wants us to live. We need to rightly order our lives to live in this fullness. Our passions, desires, and will, must be re-ordered to be healthy and to find fulfillment in Christ.

Drugs can give a person a sense of well-being, but it doesn't last and because of that, a person wants more and more. Pretty soon, they think they must have it to survive. So, it is all kinds of attachments that hinder our relationship with God. "Why do you spend your money for that which is not bread, and your labor for what does not satisfy?" (Isaiah 55:2) Only the Lord satisfies and brings fulfillment. In the Middle East water where Jesus lived, water was very precious because it largely was a desert setting. If a person drank contaminated water, they could die if they continue to drink that water or be very sick. Jesus said he would give us living water. Water gushing up to eternal life. We can choose the living water or the contaminated water.

The seven deadly sins within greatly hinder our relationship with God, others, and ourselves. Again, these sins are pride, anger or wrath, jealousy, envy, greed, lust, and gluttony. These sins cannot be rooted out simply by our will or discipline, they must also be transformed and this can only happen by God's intervening grace and because we truly want God more than we want to sin. God will make us aware of the many various forms these sins can take in our life and as God points them out to us, we must confess them and ask God to transform us in Christ. Oftentimes we make progress, but the devil is very subtle in how these sins are disguised. Sometimes Satan even pretends he is God and directs us to do something religious out of pride or leads us into spiritual pride or spiritual gluttony. (2 Corinthians 11:14)

People, don't take a lot of other things with them when they are running the race because if they do, it is unlikely they will win or perhaps finish. They may be crushed under the load. As the scriptures state, "Since we are surrounded by so great a cloud of witnesses, let us lay aside every weight and the sin which so easily ensnares us, and let us run with endurance the race that is set before us" (Hebrews 12:1). The Apostle Paul also says, "I press toward the goal for the prize of the upward call of God in Christ Jesus" (Philippians 3:14). The upward call is the fullness of positional union with God in Christ, which occurs when we are born again and walking in the practical union in Christ and which results in full union with God.

Leaving behind attachments is very important and God will reveal these to us as we draw near to Him. Not a condemnation, but as the way of physician leading us in wholeness, freedom, and fulness. Satan comes to attack our personhood and bring condemnation against us; God comes to point out areas and perspectives that need re-ordering. "Be transformed by the renewing of your mind" (Romans 12:1). Transforming the mind in its natural course will also lead to the renewing of our hearts and vice versa.

One of the greatest attachments we have is to the old self. But you might say, "Aren't we supposed to love ourselves?" Yes, we are. We would never choose God and his grace if we didn't love ourselves. Choosing Christ is most sensible and beneficial. It is the way of wisdom. Even the alcoholic, the criminal, and those completely irresponsible and destructive love themselves, even though they must also deal with self-contempt because of their actions and motives. The problem is that they don't love themselves in a healthy way. However, man's problem is that he loves himself too much. He loves himself more than he loves God or others. Selfishness is a common problem in our culture and there is little hope for change if it is celebrated, honored, and proposed as the way to health, even in the therapeutic relationship in counseling. "He who has completely uprooted self-love from his heart will, with God's help, easily conquer all the other passions. A man dominated by self-love is under the power of his passions as well, since from it arise anger, irritation, rancor, love of pleasure, and licentiousness. By self-love, we mean an impassioned disposition towards and love for the body, and the fulfillment of carnal desires."[2]

We need to love God and love Him much more than the old self if we are to experience wholeness. Being transformed in Christ is to grow in the breadth and depth of our love for God. To love God is to have our life re-ordered in the way of righteousness. To love God also equips us to love ourselves rightly and there to love others the way God loves us, or at least to grow in that love, for God's love can never be totally matched. We must also learn to "Love God, not the experience."[3] We must learn to love God.

Many people are too attached to the old self to grow in sanctified practical union with Jesus. We spend too much looking at the old self and not enough time looking at Jesus. Even those who have inferiority issues have the same problem. As we spend more time looking at Jesus, we will become less inferior in relationship to others.[4] Sometimes inferiority can be a subtle form of pride as well. Focus on loving Jesus even before loving others. We often get this backward. The tendency is to think if we love others, then

God will love us. We need to focus on the grace of God's love first and then we will not only have the love of God, but we will also love others with God and in God. Then we will have the freedom to rightly love ourselves in Christ and for the sake of Christ.

As we deal with these issues of attachments, we must be careful also that we don't become scrupulous. To be scrupulous means that we are overly concerned about every detail of our life. We examine our lives with too large a microscope. Again, focus on God and our love relationship with Him rather than ourselves. We also need to practice grace with ourselves and forgive ourselves as God forgives us. Keep our focus on the main factor—and He is it. Augustine, in his book the City of God, said it radically this way: "These two cities were made by two loves; the earthly city by the love of self and the contempt of God, and the heavenly city by the love of God and the contempt of self."

Fasting is a very good spiritual discipline to learn not to be run by bodily appetites but to be in control of these appetites to the glory of God. It also helps us focus on God and get in touch with the longing God has put in our hearts for himself and all that is good and beautiful. Fasting shows our absolute, resolute focus on God. This spiritual discipline, combined with the prayer Jesus said, has great power. (Matthew 17:21) We deny ourselves so that we might focus on God with greater intensity. (Luke 22:44)

Sometimes we may think that our attachments are such a small matter that certainly God would overlook and not make any difference. We, however, don't see the whole picture as does God and he thinks it is important to forsake, and so should we. At other times we may compare ourselves to others and think if it is alright for them, then it must be for us. However, as we know, each of us is unique and we should be listening to God to guide us. St. John of the Cross says in his book, *The Ascent of Mount Carmel*, "It makes little difference whether a bird is tied by a thin thread or by a cord. For even if tied by a thread, the bird will be prevented from taking off as surely as it were tied by cord... This is the lot of a man who is attached to something no matter how much virtue he has, he will not reach the freedom of the divine union."[5] "The total correction of all the appetites is not attained until a soul reaches union with God. What grieved St. John was the thought that those who had received the grace to become detached from so much should afterward fail in some smaller things, which God wanted them to overcome for love of him since these trifling things can, in fact, impede so much."

Consider all that Saint Francis of Assisi had forsaken. The Lord impressed him with this verse that Jesus stated to the rich young man, "If you want to be perfect, go, sell your possessions and give to the poor, and you will have treasure in heaven. Then come, follow me" (Matthew 19:21). Francis gave away everything and followed the Lord. His father, who was a wealthy merchant, was upset with his approach to life and insisted that even the clothes he wore were his Father's. Francis removed all of his clothes in front of the Father and church leaders and walked into a life of simplicity. He took a vow of poverty, celibacy, and obedience to Christ. He begged in the streets for food. Thankfully someone gave him some clothes. He had no outward attachments and as he progressed, he experienced great purity of heart, his heart was filled with an enormous, passionate love for Jesus himself. Some might do this to gain attention or others because they want to be successful, Francis did it because of his passionate love for Jesus.

Not everyone is asked by the Lord to follow the same way Francis was, but Francis became a very saintly person and many joined him and still continue to do so through the Franciscan order. Money and possession have been a stumbling block for many in finding the Lord in salvation and or in Christian growth in full union with God. (Luke 12:18-20) Oftentimes, we think that the Lord can have everything, but we will be in charge of the money. How can we be in full union with him if we are so attached to money, our time, and resources? This is one of the hardest attachments to give to the Lord. Jesus often spoke about the issue of money and how it may hinder people in salvation or advancing in the Lord. (Matthew 6:24; 1 Timothy 6:9) As God's people, we are stewards of the resources God has given us and are at the disposal of the Lord, primarily to advance his kingdom. There is freedom in finding a life of simplicity or in giving to the Lord and his work.[6] There is much that money can assist the Lord's work in building churches, mission work, work of mercy and evangelism, and discipleship.

Even our relationship with our spouse must be rightly ordered. The spouse must never take the place of God. It should be dominated by love or manipulation like with human nature is far too common. It should not be a struggle to see who gets their way, but how both can add to their relationship together, in the spirit of Christ within. (1 Corinthians 7:3-5) Saint John of the Cross said, "Where there is no love, pour in love, and you shall draw out love."[7]

Asceticism is to deny the old self to make room for God. Spiritual disciplines have the idea of forsaking attachments to make time for God. Fasting would be considered an ascetic practice. Of course, some through the ages have made this an end in itself and fallen into some form of spiritual pride, yet there is great benefit from spiritual disciplines.[8] Ascetic practices are primarily when we co-operate with God by his grace to grow spiritually and in closeness to him. It is deliberately denying self to make room and time for God.

"Maturity means self-denial rather than self-enhancement. Maturity does not require the asceticism of the spiritual rigorist who believed that we must deny or even crush the self through disciplines of self-flagellation: rather, the maturity we desire involves taking off the clothes of the fallen self, as Paul describes in Colossians 2:11."[9]

"So, does God want you to enjoy life and take pleasure in it? Most certainly. But he wants your pleasure to be of the highest order, the order for which you were made, the eternal delights, the spiritual delights. He does not want you to selfishly indulge in passing and finite pleasures that never fully satisfy and always leave you hungry for more. God wants you satisfied, not hungry. He wants you are rest, not always anxious. He wants your heart to be over-flowing with joy, not always craving more."[10] The closer we come in full communion, the more we experience heaven on earth, and the more we bring glory to the one who created us and fulfill our destiny.

CHAPTER 11

CONSOLATION AND
DESOLATION

Sometimes in our Christian life, we will go through consolations in the Spirit, and sometimes we will go through desolations. Consolations are when we feel very close to the Lord and we have great joy in the Lord. However, the joy is not always at the same level. We feel loved and we love the Lord. We enter into God's beauty, fullness, and goodness. Consolations, however, are not our main objective, our objective is the Lord himself, and he gives consolations as he chooses.

This consolation from the Lord ebbs and flows and can be very intense at some times and mild at others, or at times we can feel abandoned—like a dark night. Sometimes this consolation lasts a long time, coming with strength and weakness and other times, it only lasts a short time. As the psalmist says, "Taste and see the Lord is good." To experience God in His goodness is to have great consolations. We might at times have strong consolations and at other times weak consolations. (Hebrews 6:18) Whether strong or weak, the Lord is the pearl of great price. (Matthew 13:46) Of course, the pearl of great price is primarily our salvation, but for this life after being born from above by His Spirit, the pearl of great price is to be in increasingly closeness to Him.

This is how we experience the fulness of our inheritance in Christ. He is our consolation. He is what makes heaven—heaven. It takes diligence to find this pearl of great price. The spiritual disciplines make us available to God and makes room, much room for God in our lives. We battle against the devil and our selfishness and the effects of the lingering fallen nature (or as the Bible refers to it, the flesh) to draw close to Him. Some give up and settle for mediocracy and just to get by. When I was in grade school, I did just enough work to get by and get a somewhat respectful grade. To take this approach to the Lord is to miss out on the greatest blessing in this life and partly in the life to come. When I became a Christian, this changed for the most part for me.

Desolation is when we don't feel the Lord and when we feel oppressed. This oppression can be psychological, or from the evil one, or the old self, and even a withdrawing of the Lord's sense of presence, but not of himself. Satan often jumps on the band wagon, wherever the issues are presented. This is the normal experience of all Christians. Sometimes, the Lord withdraws that we might learn to walk in faith rather than just emotions, which can become an idol in themselves. Sometimes, we experience resistance from the evil one. Sometimes it is a time called the Dark Night of the Soul, which Saint John of the Cross writes about, as do many other saints. It takes practice and discernment as well as trust to distinguish in these times of desolation. This is learned by those who "have their senses exercised to discern both good and evil" (Hebrews 5:14). Satan is at the root of all desolation.

In communion with God in prayer, we will often run into ourselves, where God reveals some sin in our life. For instance, pride has many ways of disguising itself and it must be confessed and given to the Lord for cleansing and transformation. God comes to us with specific issues and inward sins, such as the seven deadly sins that have been mentioned previously. This can be quite discouraging if we think we can by our own will, change and transform ourselves. It is a work of God. We only need to agree with God, confess the specifics of the sin, and ask Him for cleansing. (1 John 1:9)

Satan comes to condemn as a person. "You never amount to anything," which may have its roots in some parental upbringing from our childhood. Satan likes to piggyback on these issues. We must reject these statements or thoughts and correct them with the truth in Christ. The devil often will try to resist us when we are advancing in the Lord. In fact, we can expect resistance when we are advancing. (Romans 7:21) If you are not a threat to Satan, he will let you be and then, at an opportune time—bring destruction or just lead you to waste your life. He will try to discourage us with lies about God and what God is doing in our lives and the lives of others. He will try to get us to focus on circumstances rather than God. He will try to get us to be discouraged and complain. He will insist that we determine what truth is entirely by the circumstances rather than by what God is saying in His Word and the Spirit. We reject all Satan's lies and distortions.

Discernment is needed. One of the spiritual gifts is the discernment of spirits. Saint Ignatius wrote a great deal about the discernment of spirits. Discernment is of critical importance, especially these days of distorted and weakened theology and lack of knowledge about spiritual theology. We learn primarily by experience, by the habitual dedication of time, and by making room for God. "My sheep hear my voice," Jesus said. (John 10:27) If my wife calls me on the phone, I don't need to ask who it is. I know her voice. So those who have learned by practice to hear God's voice. This is important because Satan tries to, at times, imitate God's voice and even get us to do religious or spiritual things out of step with God's spirit or in the spirit of pride, or we can have impressions not from the Lord. Again, we as Evangelicals have often over-simplified matters. "Therefore, because multiple forces are at work, people cannot always tell whether what they perceive to be threats come from God, from Satan, or from human sin."[1] This also applies to His direction in our lives.

Discernment has to do with discerning what is psychological, what is from the devil, and what is from God. Ignatius of Loyola said in regards to God leading us that we should pay special attention to matters of the heart as a way to discern God's will and how he is leading.[2] How is God dealing with our hearts? How is he influencing our desires, passions, and will? How do we need to align with him and resist the evil one? One very important rule he details is that we are under desolation; we should not make any major changes or give up on prayer. "The rule of discernment is clear: we do not choose in desolation: we do not act when our hearts are inclined toward anger, discouragement, fear, or any sense of spiritual malaise."[3] "Desolation is a sign of the evil spirit working; thus, we should never make or change a decision in desolation unless we want the devil as our spiritual director."[4]

There are various views on discerning the will of God. The book, *How Should We Choose*, edited by Douglas S. Huffman, deals with three approaches, and they are laid out in contrast to each other. The first is the blueprint approach written by Henry and Richard Blackaby. This approach says there is basically one will of God laid out for us in all circumstances and for almost everything and you can find it and fully align with God in it. It is the blueprint approach because there is only one perfect will for everyone and we arrive at that understanding by impressions in the mind that God gives us. Their perspective is good when it comes to emphasizing listening to God, but this approach, in my view, is far too simplistic and can be harmful if we are not discerning in what we perceive to be God's leading. Much discernment needs to be emphasized and how to go about it. We often just need to go through the process with God as he leads us step by step. This approach says it doesn't focus on circumstances and then, on the other hand, says circumstances play a big part. The blueprint approach has some good biblical perspectives but is lacking in its full presentation and understanding. It approaches the finding of God's will as if God would always speak to us as he did Moses and Abraham and others. Sometimes God does this, but this is often not the case.

The second approach is the way of wisdom, as presented by Garry Friesen. In this approach, we just make wise Biblical decisions based on the principles and ethics of the Bible. However, in this approach, often the leading of the Holy Spirit as he influences our mind, heart, and will is left out or underestimated. Of course, this is a factor in discerning God's will. This is helpful in for instance choosing who to marry because God's word states we are only to marry in the Lord (1 Corinthians 7:39), but it doesn't state which specific person to marry. This is where discernment is needed. The third approach that has been developed through the ages is the Learning to listen to God as clarified by Gordon T. Smith.[5] Smith deals with some of the influence of the saints of old and especially Ignatius of Loyola in discerning God's leading and his will and is a much more balanced approach. Ignatius has 14 rules he lays out for discerning the leading of the Lord and 8 greater rules for greater discernment.

With Ignatius, there are three overall guiding principles for discerning God's will. First that in seeking God's will, we are seeking the best and that God wants the best for us. Sometimes the best is sacrificed for what is just good or the lesser than best. Second, God guides us in peace. This peace must be from God and not a false peace from the evil one or a justification of sin. Third, this peace must be tested. There should also be humility in discerning God's will. It is best to say, "As best as I can tell, God is leading in this way."[6]

The danger is to oversimplify and distort how God works in our lives and underestimate the need for discernment. This is especially important because Satan often tries to imitate the voice of God and get us to do things that might be religious or spiritual but often are not in God's will or timing or distortions of what God wants to do. "For even Satan disguises himself as an angel of light" (2 Corinthians 11:14). Too often spiritual matters are disguised in pride. We also need to be aware of God's timing and his process.

Because of the complexity of recognizing God's voice at times, saints through the ages have sought out spiritual directors to walk alongside them in their journey with God. These people are familiar with the process of spiritual formation and, through experience with God, can assist others. Great discernment is needed when contacting someone to be your spiritual director. Lately, this has become a great movement among evangelicals in the United States of America. However, there are various Christian approaches to spiritual direction.

Someone wanting a spiritual director must be extremely serious about growing in union with Christ. They must have studied spiritual formation and be ones who greatly practice the life of prayer. Those involved in spiritual direction usually meet for an hour once a month. The spiritual directors must have journeyed further along the road of a full union in Christ and know where they are going and, therefore, can lead others. However, it is difficult to find a good spiritual director.

Great stumbles can occur from not understanding the process of spiritual formation by God into full union with Him. Some people might go through a time of aridity where God seems distant, and we can think that God has abandoned us or may think that they are overrun in some way by evil. Of course, there is a need for discernment here, for outward sin can also hinder our advancement and the quality of our relationship with God. People may at these times give up on God and their spiritual growth. They may coast or fall into grievous sin. This is why it is so important to know the spiritual formation process that God often takes his people through. During times of aridity, we just continue on and continue to pray and make room for God in our lives. It is wise to understand how God shapes us and learn from those who have gone before us, it will avoid much heartache and distortions. It is important to know not only systematic theology well but also spiritual theology and to hold them in a Godly balance. Of course, the Spirit will not lead us to do anything against that is revealed in the word of God.

Dan Burke, in his excellent book, *Navigating the Interior Life*, gives a very important illustration of the dangers of not being familiar with how God works in bringing full union with Christ, practically and experientially. He tells about a time he went fishing and as he was walking to the river with his gear, he noticed cougar tracks in the mud. He thought better of fishing and returned to his cabin because with his back turned to the forest and the sound of the river, he would never be prepared for a cougar attack. Similarly, we can have a lot of blind spots as it relates to ourselves and the process of spiritual formation and can be attacked in very subtle and distorted ways by the devil leading us to misunderstand and foolishness not understanding how God is working. (Proverbs 11:4) That is why it is very good for us to learn about the process and to learn and practice prayer and spiritual formation. Education in spiritual formation is very beneficial. However, our main guide is always the Holy Spirit—God himself. As Jesus said, "But the Helper, the Holy Spirit, whom the Father will send in my name, he will teach you all things and I will bring to remembrance all that I have said to you" (John 14:26).

CHAPTER 12

DARK NIGHT OF THE SOUL

Mother Teresa sensed God had abandoned her after she experienced some incredible visions and locutions. In fact, she experienced the dark night of the soul for 50 years, while in active ministry. By the way, this is the way to respond to the dark night of the soul—stay the course. Continue on with what you sensed God had led you to do. I would think that not many experience the dark night of the soul for this long. "According to their own experience, the greatest of Christian saints were also the most profoundly abandoned by God."[1] In this experience, we still have a sense of fullness but a great longing to sense the presence of the Lord, in a powerful way, perhaps in a way previous experienced. A way that is a sense of great closeness to the Lord. This will increase our thirst for the Lord and increase our faith and love for the Lord, as well.

In the normal course of spiritual formation, there are two dark nights to go through. There is the transition from beginner to proficient in the dark night of the senses and the transition from the proficient to the unitive way in the dark night of the spirit. The difference between the two purgations, St. John says, "is like the difference between pulling up the roots and cutting of the branches.[2] The dark night of the senses is the cutting of the branches and the pulling up of the roots is the dark night of the spirit. Saint John of the cross likens the dark night as when one gets very close to the sun and is overwhelmed by the brightness and one's vision shuts down and becomes dark. The light overwhelms us and truly we enter fully into all the God is and is truly magnificent but mysterious and that we don't understand all the God is doing within, and how he is purging us and giving us his grace to be fully transformed in his image. "The nearer the soul comes to God, the greater is her experience of his absence. This void is like a spiritual fire "which dries up and purges here so that thus purified she may be united to Him."[3]

However, it is especially during this dark night that God purifies us, illuminates us, transforms, stretches us, and builds our faith. Often God is doing a work we are not completely aware of, but it is especially important to His work in and through us. "Beloved, do not think it strange concerning the fiery trial which is to try you, as though some strange thing happened to you; but rejoice to the extent that you partake of Christ's sufferings, that when His glory is revealed, you may also be glad with exceeding joy" (1 Peter 4:12-13). We also share in Christ's suffering on the cross when it seemed like the Father abandoned Him on the cross. "For this light momentary affliction is preparing for us an eternal weight of glory beyond all comparison" (2 Corinthians 4:17).

God does not want us to run primarily on feelings but on love for Him and trust in Him. "Prayer is a pilgrimage. The closer I get to the goal, the further away I might feel. The more holy I become, the less holy I know myself to be."[4] Our mind is very important in relating to God, but as Theologians of the heart, our heart is the root of who we are, although the mind influences the heart and vice versa. "However, sublime may be the knowledge God gives the soul in this life, it is but a glimpse of Him from a great distance."[5]

The dark night can also be referred to as going through aridity. We sense a dryness in our relationship with God, almost as if He has abandoned us. Perhaps as Jesus felt on the cross when He cried out, "My God, My God, why have you forsaken Me?" (Matthew 27:46). After all, if we are going to follow Jesus, we must go through what He went through, although not to the same degree and certainly not as God. This certainly goes contrary to the popular health, success, and wealth gospel of today and the orientation towards the old self that, unfortunately, is promoted in some churches.

Going through the dark night can be like going through the desert. The children of Israel, with Moses as the leader, went through the wilderness. It was intended to build their faith, but instead, they refused to enter the promised land. We can whine and complain and look back to bondage as the children of Israel did, or we can keep our gaze on Him. "Today, if you hear His voice, do not harden your hearts as in the rebellion, in the day of the trial in the wilderness, where your Fathers put me to the test, and proved Me, and saw My works forty years" (Hebrews 3:7-9). "Therefore, since a promise remains of entering His rest, let us fear lest any of you seem to have come short of it" (Hebrews 4:1). Our full rest is in Christ.

The rest we are to enter into in this life is full union with Christ, in practice, by being transformed into His likeness. The rest is the enjoyment of an intimate love relationship with Him and the fulfillment that He brings. To enter his rest is to enter the promised land. "The initial impetus for the movement is a wound of love, a very painful "absence of God" which impels the soul to go out of self in search of the beloved."[6] Absence makes us want to draw even closer to God, refines our faith, and purifies us to be in a very close full union with God. "Since disordered self-love is a root obstacle to union with God, it can not be cured in no other way than by entering the night."[7]

John of the Cross said, "Aristotle and the theologians assert, the higher and more sublime the divine light, the darker it is to our intellect."[8] This is especially hard for people with strong control issues. We want to know everything. Jesus said to His disciples,

"I still have many things to say to you, but you cannot bear them now" (John 16:12). How often this is the case with us. We want to know everything and we want to know it now, and often without any sustained effort. We want to put it on the roof without first building the foundation. We are impatient and demanding. It is built brick upon brick, stone upon stone. (Isaiah 28:10) So, it is with Systematic Theology and Spiritual Theology—the theology of the heart, or the experience of God within. Let us remember that God amazingly is unfathomable in His full dimension, but we can grow in understanding in both head and heart, "what is the width and length and depth and height—to know the love of Christ which passes knowledge; that you may be filled with all the fullness of God" (Ephesians 3:18-19) In the dark night we learn to let God be God and are aware of what we don't know and the misconceptions we carry.

Today people want to learn Biblical knowledge and Spiritual Theology in one sentence. They want quick answers—after all, they are important people with stuff to do. Whoops—I just got a text. Seriously, it takes time to learn. It takes concentrated effort and deep thinking with the head and heart. Truth, at times, can seem like a wrestling match, like Jacob's experience with the angel of God, but it is greatly worth it. (Genesis 30:22-32) It is a long devotion and discipline in the same direction, with our eyes focused on the prize—Jesus.

God can not explain everything to us right now, we are not ready. There has to be more foundational experience and truth for us to be ready. Often, He will increase our desire for Him by seemingly withdrawing from us. When this happens, we can pursue Him even more, or we can be discouraged and just get by. Too often, people just end up going through the motions rather than experiencing the fullness God has planned for them. There is the temptation of the evil one to fall short. This especially happens when people have not learned the process of spiritual formation. Those who are coming to fullness, experience what the Psalmist declares when he says, "As the deer pants, for the water brooks, so pants my soul for You, O God" (Psalm 42:1).

This is not for the weak of heart, as John of the Cross says, "The dark night experience of spiritual passage resembles the unpleasant and difficult experience of the birth canal."[9] He also explains the dark night as when the wood in the fire turns black, just before bursts into flame. We become one in the flame, although we are still distinct. The dark night is largely a time of purification of the heart. When we look at God and His purity, we are in sharp contrast. The beauty is that God infuses his righteousness in us in the practical process of sanctification.

Some people see themselves and run from themselves and settle into an illusion of self, so they can have some form of human self-esteem, even if it is not true. It makes them feel better about themselves and to them, this is what counts. Our self-esteem comes primarily from the love of God. In the security of his love, we can face the truth, even about sin. However, seeing ourselves in God's light gives us the opportunity to confess to God, and ask Him for His grace to be transformed into Christlikeness. God does with us what we are not able to do by will or reformation. Of course, we must co-operate with Him in truth. "God humbles the soul greatly in order to exalt it greatly afterward."[10]

To be free from sin, the flesh, and Satan, we must be purified. Adrian Rogers said, "To try to resist Satan with pride in the heart would be no more effective than arguing with Niagara Falls in the hope of stopping the water. "Almighty God himself resists the proud person." (James 4:6)

But it is more of just purification of the heart. It is growth in knowing and loving Him. It is enlarging our love for Him in our minds and heart. Knowledge can change us or pre-empt God's change in us, but we must be transformed deep within, at the core of our being and only God can do this.

When Jesus encountered Peter during His resurrection appearances, Peter had failed His Lord and himself when he denied knowing Christ when Jesus was arrested and being taken to the cross. Jesus asked Peter, "Do you love me as I love?" Peter said, "Lord, I love you like a friend." Jesus again said, "Peter, do you love me like I and the Father love?" Peter, was a little taken back, said "Yes, Lord, you know I love you like a friend." The third time Jesus said, "Peter, do you love me like a friend?" Peter, greatly taken back, said, "You know I love you as a friend."

In the original Greek language that the New Testament was written in there were four words for love. There was storge which a family has love for one another, there is eros which is a romantic love that a couple would have in a marriage, then there is philios which is a brotherly or friendship love and then there is agape which is God's kind of love in fullness—an unmerited love. Some describe agape as unconditional love, but it is an oversimplified explanation because God's love is a perfect balance of grace and justice. It is unmerited love. The final time Jesus asked Peter if he loved him, loved as God loved. There some form of mutuality with our love towards God.

Our love for God can be at various levels. We can experience God's love in His fullness. This is God's plan for us. We can grow in that love. This is also part of the process of the dark night of the soul. Again, this is the primary objective and the fruit comes from this root. Too often, we want the fruit while having no firm root or foundation. Those we love, we enjoy.

The dark night of the soul is a mystery. It has to be experienced and it is experienced by developing a life of prayer. When we go through the dark night, we obtain the prize, which is God himself. This objective is developed by making God our first priority in our hearts as well as our minds. It comes by dedicating our time and energy to making room for Him, much room in our lives. "Without faithfulness to prayer, giving priority to God risks being nothing more than a good intention, or even an illusion. If we do not pray, we will subtlety but surely put our own egos at the center of our lives, instead of the living God."[11]

In the process, we also should not be focused on the process rather than on Him. We don't have to understand everything about the process, and we won't. God is oftentimes working and we don't know it until later, sometimes much later. Our focus is to be on Jesus. "If we look into the light of God's purity, we will come to a place where we see less, not more, the brightness creates darkened sight."[12]

John of the Cross was thrown in prison in a cell 10 x 6 for over eight months. Some of his fellow monks in the same order as him thought that Teresa of Avila and John were going too far in the reformation of the order. There he was left alone with God and there, he wrote his well know poem, the Spiritual Canticle. After eight months, he escaped. There he experienced the dark night physically, but there he spent much time in solitude with God. I myself spent 5 months in the hospital during an illness, and there I spent a lot of time in prayer and seeking God. Through that experience, it brought me closer to God, but *circumstances are not the dark night*, though they lead to a dark spiritual night. The dark night is the spiritual working of God deep within.

Solitude and silence are very necessary for prayer. Just presenting ourselves to God in prayer means that God is working in our lives, whether we realize it or not. There, however, can be different times of the dark night of the soul as God sees fit. During these times, stay the course. Continue your time of Bible reading and study and, of course, prayer. God will take you and me through the wilderness to the promised land. Just like the people of Israel who had to fight to live in the promised land, so there is a fight against the devil, the flesh, and the world for us to enter spiritually —to enter his rest fully. (1 John 2:16)

PART THREE

THE ACTIVE AND CONTEMPLATIVE LIFE

CHAPTER 13

THE CONTEMPLATIVE LIFE

"Blessed are the pure in heart, for they shall see God"
(Matthew 5:8).

I guess one danger of being a contemplative is that you just want to spend so much time with God that you avoid involvement in your world. You might rather spend time with God than with others. Many of the saints of old were metaphorically drug from the monastery to minister in and through the church. One of the great mystical experiences of Jesus and his disciples Peter, James, and John was the transfiguration on a Mountain. "And after six days, Jesus took Peter, James, and John, his brother, and led them up on a high mountain by themselves. And he was transfigured before them and his face shone like the sun, and his clothes became as white as light. And behold, there appeared to them, Moses and Elijah, talking with Him. And Peter said to Jesus, "Lord, it is good for us to be here. If You wish, I will make here three tents here, one for you, one for Moses, and one for Elijah." He was still speaking when behold, a bright cloud overshadowed them and a voice came from the cloud, said, "This is My beloved Son, in whom I am well pleased; listen to Him!" (Matthew 17:1-5).

Peter just wanted to honor Jesus and Moses and Elijah. Peter suggested building tents, just staying and soaking in this beautiful presence of God. This would be the greatest, Peter must have thought, let us just stay here. Jesus, however, had other plans for them at that time. When they came down from the Mount, they encountered a boy who was demon-possessed and his other disciples were trying to cast out a demon but were unable. Jesus immediately cast the demon out and the boy was healed. (Mark 9:14-29) Jesus said to them, "This kind can come out by nothing but prayer and fasting" (Mark 9:29 NKJV). Jesus had a relationship with the Father that prepared him for ministry. Are we also prepared for ministry by spending valuable time with God? Fasting symbolizes and practices being free from attachments before God and being completely a channel that God can bless through. Fasting is an act of dedication and devotion to God.

Everyone's timing for ministry is different. We need to value time with God above everything else before we are truly ready and continue to be ready for ministry. We need to learn to have a life dedicated to him in prayer. As mentioned, it is not for the faint of heart. It is a difficult road. Few may be on this road.

It is interesting that specifically that Moses and Elijah were chosen to be with Jesus on the Mount of transfiguration. Moses spent 40 years in the desert before being called by God to ministry. He, however, did not lead God's people ultimately into the promised land, because in anger, he took the glory of God for Himself. (Numbers 20:11-12) Moses' protégé Joshua took God's people into the promised land. However, in spite of Moses' failure, he was in the promised land at the transfiguration on Mount with Jesus. Elijah ministered in a time of apostasy and then, by God's grace, was taken up to heaven without dying and Elisha, who he had mentored, continued on in the Lord's ministry, calling God's people back to the Lord. Both Moses and Elijah had a very close relationship with the Lord. "Of all the prophets through the millennium of Israel's history, only two had physically stood in the presence of great manifestation of the glory of God. Then they stood again in that presence when Christ was transfigured before them."[1] They both were honored in a special way at the Mount of transfiguration. Like them, every person has the potential to have a very close relationship with God.

It is good to want God more than anything else. This qualifies us and equips us for ministry, not only in the short haul but in the long road of faithfulness and love for God. We do need schools dedicated to spiritual formation, retreat centers, and shared community life dedicated to a life of prayer. Places that are at least somewhat secluded from the noise of the world and dedicated to the Lord. In today's world, some instruction may also be given online. We also need seminaries strongly rooted in spiritual formation, as well as Theology. People think they can learn spiritual formation in a couple of semesters, but as in all good things, it takes time. God is not so concerned about you being successful as much as he wants you to be close to Him—and to fully bear his image and fullness. This is what it means to be successful in Christ. It may take years to grow in the learning of spiritual formation. It took Moses 40 years in a desert before he recognized the burning bush. (Exodus 3:1-4) Some Catholic seminaries have students spend the first year in prayer and learning spiritual formation.

Many things in the spiritual realm are counterintuitive, which is why it takes so long to learn. Consider Jesus' sermon on the mount. These matters go against our sinful passions. That is why prayer is partly a battle. My wife and I like to go for a ride on our

ATV. Going up hills, the natural inclination is to lean back, but this is exactly the wrong thing to do. We need to both lean forward to keep the weight to the front so the ATV, going up steep hills, does not flip over. The consequence of not doing this could be disastrous. So those who follow their natural self, the results can be tragic. We need to lean strongly into God. We need to do what is natural in Christ.

However, practicing contemplative prayer and progressing in closeness to God is not just for the monks. It is for everyday people, the doctor, the lawyer, the police, the military, and administrators and laborers. Everyone can make God first and be progressing in closeness to Him, making wise use of their time. Unless Bible study and prayer are a priority, it is unlikely we will make much progress, if any. Jesus said, "You shall love the Lord your God with all your heart, with all your soul, and with all your mind" (Matthew 22:37). Notice the progression—heart, soul, and then mind. We have reversed the order. We have enlarged the head and neglected the heart. In other words, love the Lord with all your affections as well as your mind. We can never outdo God's love, but we can seek to be responsible and come close to matching it. We can grow in that love as He transforms us. We can co-operate with him in making ourselves available to Him and His transforming grace.

The story is told about a Bishop that was visiting various monasteries to evaluate their spiritual health. On his way back to where he was stationed, he had one last stop. It was a deserted island that had 5 monks living on it. He found out that they didn't have many manuscripts of scripture and that they didn't even know the Lord's prayer. He spent all night teaching them the Lord's prayer, for he needed to embark the next day.

· · ·

As he sailed away, he felt pretty good about himself, for the monks had sent him off thanking him profusely. After they sailed for about an hour, he was shocked to see in the distance on the ocean a very odd sight, that he couldn't quite make out. As the objects came closer, he was amazed to see the 5 monks running on top of the ocean water toward the ship. As they came to the side of the ship, they were in great remorse and asked the bishop to spend more time with them, for they had forgotten the Lord's prayer. Could he teach them again?

Yes, theological knowledge is of great knowledge, but knowledge and experiences of the heart are equally important. He must touch our heart and give us a new heart in salvation and a new heart as we are progressively transformed in Christlikeness, out of the fullness of union with Him. We will then walk close to Him. We must go beyond knowing him to also deeply loving him, as he does us.

A peasant man used to constantly come to church and sit for hours in one of the pews. A priest decided one day to approach him and ask if he could be of assistance. The man said, no, he was just praying." The priest wanting to explore further, said, "Can I pray with you about something?" The man said, "No, I just gaze at Jesus and He gazes at me."

This is a good illustration of what contemplative prayer is. It is being with Jesus, largely in silence. It is truly enjoying Him and letting him enjoy being with us, as we contemplate Him and dialogue with Him. He is the initiator and we are the responder. Of course, this only happens when we make much room and take time for Him—much time and room. He must be our priority and prayer is the way we most importantly make Him our priority. Prayer is the channel to make ourselves available to Him. A life not spent in prayer is a life choosing not to breathe. It is to miss out on life's greatest blessing—Himself.

God addresses the church at Ephesus in the book of Revelation, chapter 2. He commends the church for dealing with right doctrine and exposing false teachers, but He states, "Nevertheless I have this against you, that you have left your first love" (Revelation 2:4). Theologians have debated what this first love is that He is referring to here. I believe it somewhat obvious considering the rest of the Bible that this first love referred to here is God Himself. They have the right doctrine and stand up to the error, but they have not nurtured their love for God and their hearts are not being enlarged in their capacity to love Him. What we don't nurture is weakened.

Prayer is the gateway to communion with God and intimacy with Him. Prayer is the way to spend time with God and nurture our relationship with Him and be transformed into His likeness. Too often, we think we can transform ourselves and that is impossible, at least to the root of our being—to the inner man. (Ephesians 3:16) "The passivity into which the Lord eventually leads us in prayer is so contrary to our natures, and the world into which we enter is so "upside down," that it seems the same lesson needs to be learned a thousand times over before it becomes truly our own."[2]

Jesus says to the church at Ephesus that if they don't repent of their loss of their first love, He will come and remove their lampstand. (Revelation 2:5) A church that doesn't teach Theology and Spiritual Theology and thus prayer and spiritual formation is weak and they are not then teaching full dimensions of discipleship.

. . .

If we are truly Christian, we have a love relationship with Him, but many do not have a close relationship with Him. It is primarily a user-friendly relationship. God does things for us and we serve Him. It is largely transactional in many Christian's minds. We bargain with Him, and if He doesn't meet our expectations of Him, we are disappointed.

In Eugene Peterson's book, *Run with the Horses,* he gives this illustration of what many perceive prayer as and our relationship to God. A friend wants to take you out to dinner and a very nice restaurant of your choice. You pick the restaurant and you and he is tremendously enjoying your conversation and the meal together. The meal is very good, but the waiter is meeting all your expectations. You think that you will not leave much of a tip.

The friend you are having dinner with is yourself, and the waiter is God. Often times we think that God is here to serve us and meet our expectations, rather than for us to serve Him and to grow in our love relationship with Him. Our perspective is quite wrong and very unhealthy. It is detrimental to truly knowing God and to truly loving Him and becoming our true selves in Him.

We are transformed by time spent with Him. We may not realize the changes, but God is working on transforming us, even when we don't realize it. It is often said that children spell love T.I.M.E. So for married couples. Developing a love relationship to the full takes time with God. Nothing will replace time spent with God. This occurs when we make ourselves available to Him with great devotion. "One sure mark of genuine spiritual growth, I think, is a growing preference for the ordinary days of our life with God. We gradually begin to realize that it is when nothing seems to be happening that the most important things are really taking place."[3]

. . .

Too often, pride and insecurity get in our way. Pride and insecurity can often overlap and contaminate one another. Where are the springs of living water that Jesus promised? (John 7:38) Too often, we are not experiencing the abundant life Jesus promised. (John 10:10) This is because we have largely neglected Him. The way of fullness in this life is part of the pearl of great price that is Christ Himself. In the process, He calls us to our true selves in Christ and the peace and contentment that is found only in Him. This only happens when we spend quality and valuable time with Him.

We can stop short of that fullness; we can choose not to nurture the longings of our hearts and truly do ourselves and others harm. We experience the fulness of life in conversion and thus salvation, but we are to go on to experience the full dimensions of that fullness by growing in our love relationship with Him.

CHAPTER 14

THE CONTEMPLATIVES THAT
HAVE GONE BEFORE US

**"Let a man so consider us, as servants of Christ and
stewards of the mysteries of God" (1 Corinthians 4:1).**

Before we look at the distortions, let us consider the people of
prayer who have gone before us. There are many contemplatives in the Old Testament. Just to mention a few, there were
Adam and Eve; Noah, Abraham, Jacob, David, Solomon, Elijah,
Elisha, and the rest of the prophets. Each encountered God in the
Spirit or had visions or dreams from God. Jesus was certainly
contemplative, as he spoke directly from immediate and
prolonged conversations with God. (Matthew 14:23) The Apostles were men of prayer and they had a close relationship with
Him even after Jesus was no longer on earth physically. The
Apostle Paul describes some of his mystical experiences. "I know a
man in Christ who fourteen years ago was caught up to the third
heaven—whether in the body I do not know, or whether out of
the body I do not know, God knows. And I know that this man
was caught up to into paradise—whether in the body or out of
the body I do not know, God knows—and he heard things that

cannot be told, which man may not utter" (2 Corinthians 12:2-4). It has been said by some historical scholars that even Martin Luther had a similar experience. John the elder of John the Apostle, who wrote Revelation, was most certainly a Christian mystic. "I was in the Spirit on the Lord's Day, and I heard behind me a loud voice, as of a trumpet" (Revelation 1:10). And I saw a new heaven and a new earth, for the first heaven and first earth had passed away. Also, there was no more sea" (Revelation 21:1). The gospel of John certainly especially is contemplative, as well as the book of Ephesians. This Biblical basis should be enough to show us the value of Christian prayer and full union with God.

The prophet Joel prophesied this for the coming New Covenant in Christ, "And it shall come to pass afterward that I will pour out My Spirit on all flesh; Your sons and daughters shall prophesy, your old men shall dream dreams, your young men shall see visions, and also on My menservants and on My maidservants, I will pour My Spirit in those days" (Joel 2:28-29).

However, God today doesn't usually speak to us audibly or through visions and dreams, but He can and does at times. Most usually, He speaks to us and guides us through our mind, will, and heart. This is a process God must see great value in. There is a way that God normally works in prayer. There is great value in our spiritual formation. It does involve some struggle, but there is a great blessing in drawing close to Him through this struggle. He is the reward. He is the pearl of great price. "Again, the kingdom of heaven is like a merchant in search of fine pearls, who, on finding one pearl of great value, went and sold all that he had and bought it" (Matthew 13:45-46).

As we get to know God, we will grow in self-knowledge. That can be difficult but is also freeing. However, out of our need for union with God, we can forsake the distorted and cling to what is whole and healing. However, "the half-hearted beginner will take offenses at the severity."[1] Spiritual formation does, however, involve great and beautiful healing. To know God is also to take a look at ourselves. We run up against all that is corrupted in us in the midst of the wonderful, brilliant light of his presence and glory. We can forsake our sin and confess it to God and He will cleanse us and transform us. This only happens when we really want it. The closer we draw to God, the more we will value God and the process. The more we will get in touch with our most basic essence, which is our desire for Him, the more we will experience all that is good, even in spite of the circumstances. (Philippians 4:12-13) A good example of this is St. Therese of Lisieux in the book, *The Story of the Soul.* In the midst of her much time in sickness, she was very close to God and very saintly.

"Draw near to God and He will draw near to you. Cleanse your hands, you sinner, and purify your hearts, you double-minded. Lament and mourn and weep! Let your laughter be turned to mourning and your joy to gloom. Humble yourself in the sight of the Lord and He will lift you up" (James 4:8-10). Lament because of sin within and without, and the state of the world without Christ and the Lukewarmness of the church, but rejoice in Christ.

Satan attacks what is most valuable and often distorts it by imitation. It is no wonder that he attacks what is called spiritual formation. Many are afraid of spiritual formation and its teaching of the journey of the heart but miss out on life's greatest blessing besides their salvation in Christ. It is amazing how many different non-Christian mystic traditions there are. There are mystic traditions in Judaism known as Kabbalah, Buddhism called Zen, Islam mysticism named Sufism, Vedanta (Hindu mysticism) and shamanism (indigenous mysticism), as well as the secular new age spirituality of today. These people are seeking God and are experiencing some of the benefits of focusing on searching for God, but they are from a Christian perspective, experiencing a limited peace or stopping short of entering into the fulness that is in Christ. "They have also healed the hurt of My people slightly, saying, 'Peace, peace!' When there is no peace" (Jeremiah 6:14). They are, as Matthew Mead has stated in his book, *Almost Christians*

Discovered, users of God but don't know God. Jesus said, "Not everyone who says to me, 'Lord, Lord,' will enter the kingdom of heaven, but the one who does the will of my Father in heaven. On that day, many will say to me, 'Lord, Lord, did we not prophesy in your name, and cast out demons in your name, and do many mighty works in your name? And then will I declare to them, 'I, never knew you; depart from me, you workers of lawlessness" (Matthew 7:21-23)

As Evelyn Underhill states, Mysticism is "one of the most abused words in the English language, it has been used in different and often mutually exclusive senses by religion, poetry, and philosophy: has been claimed as an excuse for every kind of occultism, for dilute transcendentalism, vapid symbolism, religious or aesthetic sentimentality, and bad metaphysics. On the other hand, it has been freely employed as a term of contempt by those who have criticized these things. It is much to be hoped that it may be restored sooner or later to its old meaning, as the science or art of the spiritual life."[2]

Of course, there are some distortions of Christian mysticism as well. Just like a little psychology can be dangerous, so can a little mysticism if it is not Biblically and Theologically centered. Madame Guyon, in her book, *Experiencing the Depths of Jesus Christ,* is an example of some fine distortions. She overemphasized some aspects and focused on passivity (not what most contemplatives mean as divine receptivity) and the annihilation of the self to experience full union with God. She, however, remarkably influenced many, including some greats like George Whitfield, John Wesley, Fenelon, Count Zinzendorf, and the early Quakers. "Jessie Pen-Lewis and Hudson Taylor all highly recommended it to the believer of their day."[3] These people most likely sorted the wheat from the chaff in her teachings. She is not accepted by the Catholic church as a saint because of some of these concerns, maybe this is why she was so readily accepted by Protestants. However, there are many good instructions we can learn from Madame Guyon while practicing diligent discernment.

"Because evil will increase" and many become discouraged, in the last days, as the Roman Catholic Theologian Karl Rahner says, "In the day ahead, you will either be a mystic or nothing at all. The life of prayer and the contemplative life will be the only way to stay on track when the darkness keeps blanketing our culture. Jesus said, "that men always ought to pray and not lose heart" (Luke 18:1). The word of God promises we will "reap if we do not lose heart" (Galatians 6:9). Jesus said, "And because lawlessness will abound, the love of many will grow cold. But he who endures to the end will be saved" (Matthew 24:12-13). Only a vital ongoing progressive experience with God in prayer will take you through evil days.

Accordingly, A.W. Tozer said, "For millions of Christians, God is no more real than he is to non-Christians. They go through life trying to love an ideal and be loyal to a mere principle."[4]

The word mystic basically means "hidden." Is God hidden? Sometimes it seems like it. Why is God so hard to find? He is hidden because of sin, evil, and inordinate self-love and misconceptions, and desires only to use and manipulate God. I believe it is because, in the searching and the making of ourselves available to Him, He confronts us and transforms us, so that we can receive him. "The mark of a good prayer life is not abundant consolation, but growth in virtues."[5] Besides, we are not just to live our life based on feeling, but upon Him and truth. As C.S. Lewis stated, that is God's primary purpose to make us "little Christs." There is great value in the search. "Ask, and it will be given to you, seek and you will find; knock and it will be opened to you" (Matthew 7:7). This seeking of God is to be with all your soul, mind, heart, and strength. It is not a casual walk in the park or a short prayer when driving our car, but it is a concentrated and dedicated time spent before the unfathomable God in prayer. God is so big that it will take more than eternity to fathom Him.

There is a mystery in how God works in prayer, especially contemplative prayer. Until we have experienced this kind of prayer and all real Christian, have experienced it to a certain degree, when we like C.S. Lewis get in touch with our longing for God, until we experience God in ever-increasing contemplative prayer, we will be missing out on the greatest fulfillment in God in this life. A person can be a pastor and can see people coming to Christ and the church growing with great fellowship and having a good family life, but unless our prayer life is vitally in Christ, we will have missed an element in our lives. It is a God-shaped vacuum that no amount of success, family, friends, or busyness or success can fill, even outward spiritual success.

God teaches us in the silence before Him. This kind of prayer is not completely understood, nor should we focus primarily on how God does things, but upon Him. We should let Him be God in our lives and follow His lead. Yes, we may even have to go through personal suffering and suffering for the body of Christ as the apostle Paul states, "I now rejoice in my suffering for you, and fill up in my flesh what is lacking in the afflictions of Christ, for the sake of His body, which is the church" (Colossians 1:24).

Michael Molinos states, "There are two ways for the soul to be cleansed. The first is through affliction, anguish, distress, and inward torment. The second is through the fire of burning love, a love impatient and hungry."[6] Better to go through adversity and experience the Lord than to wander aimlessly through the wilderness in futility. (Matthew 5:27-30) The way to union with God is not always just an oasis, "but rather a vast desert of purifying dryness with, perhaps, occasional small oases of consolations to sustain the spirit. As we shall see, it is only when we come to love the desert and prefer it to the oases that we are well on our way to God. It is an "upside-down" world indeed! We can well be forgiven for forgetting, for refusing to believe we are on the right road when our throats are parched and our eyes are filled with sand!"[7]

God teaches us by and with the Holy Spirit. He reveals things about us and things about Him and His will. He works deep within us to root out sin and purify our hearts in Him. (Matthew 5:8) By grace, we become more like Him. "Although grace is essential for man's restoration to God, it is not poured into the soul of the adult person without his free consent."[8] This consent involves our earnest, passionate, disciplined seeking of God—the seeking of being close to Him. Are we one of His intimates? Do we want to be? If we earnestly desire God, we will draw close to Him. We need to get in touch with our foremost longing if we are in Christ, which is God.

"Likewise, the Spirit also helps in our weaknesses. For we do not know what we should pray for as we ought, but the Spirit Himself makes intercession for us with groanings which cannot be uttered. Now he who searches the hearts knows what the mind of the Spirit is because He makes intercession for the saints according to the will of God" (Romans 8:26). This is contemplative prayer. We know from the scripture that our primary calling is to be and become saints in inheritance and practice. His will is that we choose to walk in close union with Him and thus become more and more Christlike, everything else will flow out of this. This is how God is primarily glorified in our lives. Love, Faith, Hope, evangelism, missions, and ministry will all have their foundation in this primary calling. As Martin Luther stated, our focus a faith and love in Jesus Christ.

C.S. Lewis said, "He was on the foothills of the life of prayers, he did not have a head for the heights, unlike the mountaineering mystics!"[9]

Various Saints tried to describe the somewhat indescribable and to be Spiritual directors to those who would follow them as they follow Christ. As the Apostle Paul states, "Therefore I urge you, imitate me" (1 Corinthians 4:16). He didn't mean just outwardly but inwardly in His love for God and His being and becoming a saint. He also said, "Not that I have already attained, or am already perfected; but I press on, that I may lay hold of that for which Christ Jesus has also laid hold of me. Brethren, I do not count myself to have apprehended; but one thing I do, forgetting those things which are behind and reaching forward to those things which are ahead. I press toward the goal for the prize of the upward call of God in Christ Jesus" (Philippians 3:12-14).

Saint John of the Cross emphasized leaving all attachments if we were going to grow closer to Christ. Everything that is somewhat like an idol or even a good attachment that comes before God or is not rightly ordered, we must forsake or get it in right order. If we are going to climb a mountain, we don't take our 65-inch flat-screen TV with us up the mountain. If we do, it may take months, or we might just give up or die of thirst or starvation. God, through the Holy Spirit, will reveal those things that are attachments and that will hinder us. The closer we come to God, the more we will want to come close to Him. We will forsake the lesser for the greater. At the same time, we must avoid the distortion from the devil to be overly scrupulous.

Michael Horton mentions in his two-volume book on Justification that our main objective in life is union with God, as did Martin Luther, Calvin Jonathan Edwards, and John Murray. Martin Luther said, "We must be united to Christ because "all our good is outside us, and that good is Christ."[10] We come into union with God in salvation but also grow in union with God in sanctification, which is union with God in practice. We are united with Christ as Saint John of the Cross describes like a piece of wood in a fire. First, the wood heats up and the moisture escapes, then it turns black and then it burns and is united with the fire. The fire is God's burning love. God's love separates us from all distortions. The fire burns away anything that is not part of our true self, our true image of God in us, the true person we were created to be. The Contemplatives also talk about receiving the wound of love, where because we have experienced his love in fullness, we continue to progress in our love and yearning for God. In the process, we become more and more partakers of the divine nature instead of sin and thus, we become more and more Christlike. (2 Peter 1:4) John the Baptist said, "I indeed baptize you with water unto repentance, but He who is coming after me is mightier than I, whose sandals I am not worthy to carry. He will baptize you with the Holy Spirit and fire" (Matthew 3:11). The fire is God's purification process in sanctification. The fire can also be a fire that burns because, in hell, all good is withdrawn. Those who truly *do not receive* Christ in true repentance and faith, as Jesus said, will spend eternity in hell. Truly the fire that warms can burn. "For our God is a consuming fire" (Hebrews 12:29).

Teresa of Avila speaks about going through various stages or rooms in a mansion to draw close to God. Many other saints describe the stages in various ways. God works with us uniquely in each stage. It is interesting that these saints over 2000 years speak about similar processes; it seems to be the normal way that God works in our lives in general. When we say stages, we are not talking about techniques like the modern thinker who immediately tends to think. It is about us growing in a love relationship. Hopefully, like mature people, we will go on from thinking all about ourselves like children and teenagers tend to and go on to live a life filled with gratitude and love for others and especially for God. This will also involve giving sacrificially to others. One of our greatest gifts these days seems to be time—focused time spent with others. A time that hopes to add to others' lives, as well as our own. Like the Apostle, Paul states, "For I long to see you, that I may impart to you some spiritual gift, so that you may be established" (Romans 1:11). When our compassionate love overcomes fear, we will learn the gospel well enough to lead others to Christ or sow seed for others to come to Christ.

When we first come to Christ in conversion, we come because we need and want something from God—our salvation. Then we love God for what He has done. Next, we love God for who He is. Fourthly we love God because He loves all and then we love ourselves in Christ. Finally, we love God, for He is our essence by His grace. These are stages we go through, just like a baby, child, teenager, adult and senior go through. We should be moving from an orientation on self to others and the big picture. "The silver-haired head is a crown of glory if it is found in the way of righteousness" (Proverbs 16:31). There are too many silver-headed that are primarily orientated to the old self.

Saint Ignatius believed that ingratitude was the root sin of all the other sins. Ingratitude may have been what led Adam and Eve to eat of the forbidden tree, as Satan tempted their hearts with vanity and pride. If we are not grateful people, we will neglect God and thus, pride will rule our lives. Pride has many ways of hiding, even in the subtleness of spiritual pride. Gratitude is not just thanking God for what He gives us materially but for Himself and His grace in salvation and sanctification. Any good in us is because of Him. Who is getting the credit in our lives? How do we express gratitude every day? Thomas Keating said, "Nothing is more helpful to reduce pride than the actual experience of self-knowledge.

The purification process may be difficult. We don't want to look at ourselves. In the process, Satan will seek to condemn us; however, the Holy Spirit will point out issues that need to be cleansed and transformed. This is a long process, especially with the issue of pride. Stay before the Lord, He does not come to condemn us but to cleanse us. We must make a clear distinction between what is from God and what is from the devil. Satan comes to condemn; God comes to release and restore. God comes to us about issues, and Satan attacks us as people. He attacks our identity. The Old Testament gave a lot of instruction about being physically being purified to come before God in the place of worship. This is a symbol of how we need to be spiritually purified to come close to Him. In the Old Testament, the focus was on the cleansing of purifying themselves physically to enter God's presence; in the New Testament, the focus is on the cleaning of the heart. Let us come boldly to the throne of grace, that we might find grace to help in the time of need" (Hebrews 4:16). Those with a pure heart come close to him. (Psalm 24:-6)

Some of the other saints we can learn a great deal from are: Athanasius and his book the Life of Antony (a great classic), St. Therese of Lisieux, Bernard of Clairvaux, Augustine, Francis of

Assisi. Some modern Catholic writers such as Ralph Martin and his books: The *Fulfillment of All Desire, Called to Holiness, Hungry for God* and Jacques Philippe, *Time for God, In the School of the Holy Spirit, Searching and Maintaining Peace, Thirsty for Prayer.* Anthony Lilles, *Hidden Mountain, Secret Garden* and *Fire from Above,* Daniel Burke, *Navigating the Interior Life,* The books by Henri Nouwen. Eastern Orthodox writers like Vladimir Lossky, *The Mystical Theology of the Eastern Church* and Raymond Gawronski, *Word and Silence.* Then there is the Protestant classic called, *Mysticism* by Evelyn Underhill. To be celebrated and honored are the modern Evangelical authors, especially Bruce Demarest and his books: *Satisfy Your Soul* and *Soulguide* and James Houston and *The Transforming Power of Prayer; The Heart's Desire; and The Mentored Life,* Richard Foster, (classic) *Celebration of the Disciplines, Freedom of Simplicity; Money, Sex and Power, Satisfy You Soul* and *Longing for God:* Keith R. Anderson and Randy D. Reese, *Spiritual Mentoring: A Guide for Seeking and Giving Direction.* Other helpful books will be listed in the Bibliography. These will assist you as spiritual guides, and perhaps God will bless you in a mentoring relationship with one who understands the spiritual direction and as well, you can take some courses on spiritual formation. Spiritual directors are hard to find, and great discernment is needed in choosing one. Maybe you will be blessed with a spiritual friend or mentor, depending on the stage one is at.

It is wise to learn from those who have gone before us. These people, some of them spent years in the desert, seeking God. Eventually, with people like Antony of the desert, people came from everywhere to talk to these saints and find their way to Christ. Many of them, like Francis, was not just spending time with God but went boldly to the marketplace to proclaim Christ and preach the way of salvation and sanctification. They didn't hold back in instructing people also on the reality of hell and how these people needed to avoid hell at all costs. Many people saw Christ in these saints and also chose to follow Christ. Francis wasn't just a meek little man but boldly preached the gospel. Some think he actually said, go everywhere to preach the gospel and when you have to use words, but Franciscan scholars state that these are not his words. The point is that he was not only a mystic but an evangelist and one who lovingly ministered with all his might. This is the right order for ministry.

CHAPTER 15

THE ACTIVE LIFE

The contemplative life will lead to an active life. "For we are his workmanship created in Christ Jesus for good works, which God prepared beforehand, that we should walk in them" (Ephesians 2:10). "But be doers of the word, and not hearers only, deceiving yourselves. For if anyone is a hearer of the word and not a doer, he is like a man who looks intently at his natural face in the mirror. For he looks at himself and goes away and at once forgets what he was like. But the one looks into the perfect law, the law of liberty, and perseveres, being no hearer who forgets but a doer who acts, he will be blessed in his doing. If anyone thinks he is religious and does not bridle his tongue but deceives his heart, this person's religion is worthless. Religion that is pure and undefiled before God the Father is this: to visit orphans and widows in their affliction and to keep oneself unstained from the world" (James 1:22-27)

In the contemplative life, we obtain the heart of God and not only a love for God, but with God. We care for others as God cares for them. In this way, our love is not contaminated by the old self but is sincere with the love of God. The closer we draw to God, the more we desire what God desires—absolute goodness and love. Not a sentimental and shallow love of the world but love that is centered in God, his love, his strength, his grace and mercy, his truth and justice.

Jesus makes an enormous point in his parable of the unforgiving servant in Matthew 18:21-36. Here a man is forgiven millions but refuses to forgive hundreds of his fellow man. This is hypocritical and goes against the gospel. This ingratitude reveals the condition of the man's heart. The Bible talks about receiving the grace of God in vain. (1 Corinthians 15:10) We receive the grace of God in vain when we receive but do not give it to others. Forgiveness is at the heart of the gospel—even though it is not possible without God's grace, it is more than possible with and in God's grace. We are to be forgiving people and a sharing people.

Another very important way we extend grace is by giving to others the best, which is the gospel. We must proclaim the gospel so that others may understand and come to saving faith. If we refuse to share the gospel with others, no matter how difficult it is, especially these days, it is a great form of ingratitude to God. This is the Lord's heart: "not wishing that any should perish, but that all should reach repentance" (2 Peter 3:9) People are going to a horrible place called hell, Jesus tells us, if they do not receive the gift of life in Christ's substitute for their sin on the cross. However, God wants everyone to come to him—to come home to a loving Father.

If we are going to share the gospel with others, we must understand it clearly ourselves. It is one matter to understand things for ourselves; it is another to teach others. One has to know something well to teach others. We need to take time to understand and know how to communicate the gospel. The Theologian R.C. Sproul states, "What is the gospel? There is perhaps no more important question for us to answer because the answer we give will help to determine our eternal destiny. Unfortunately, there appears to be widespread ignorance today among professing evangelicals about what the gospel is. What is its content? What is the good news, why is it good news, and what does it mean to believe in the gospel of Jesus Christ? We must understand not only the origin of the gospel but the meaning of the gospel. It is urgent that we Christians get the gospel right because if we don't, we're not going to get much at all right in the understanding of the fullness of our faith in Christ."[1] However, if people don't understand the bad news that because of sin, they cannot go to heaven on their own, they must accept the provision God has provided in Jesus Christ. It makes no sense to talk about God if we don't talk about Jesus Christ.

In a study, it was found that about 2% of evangelical Christians actually explain the gospel to others. In Canada, where I live, it is probably less than 1%. "Luther warned that anytime the gospel is proclaimed boldly and with clarity, the result will be conflict." "It is that conflict that many people seek desperately to avoid. At times, we do everything we can to obscure the gospel because we're afraid that its power to introduce conflict into our church will be a negative influence on our congregation. We focus on everything except the gospel, forgetting that it is the gospel to which God has committed His power and the power of the Holy Spirit."[2] If we are not preaching and explaining the atonement, we are not preaching the gospel. The gospel does offend human pride and it is confrontational. Jesus said, "Blessed is the one who is not offended by me" (Matthew 11:6) (see also Galatians 5:11). The cross offends human pride because they think God should accept them on their terms and in their sin, without a Savior. They want to do it on their own. Anyone who truly preaches the gospel will offend human pride. However, we need not and should not do it in an offensive way. In the midst of this, Jesus said we should be as wise as serpents and innocent as doves. (Matthew 10:16) We need to approach people in wise ways although in bold and direct ways. Jesus said he will make us fishers of men. We need to cast out the lure without compromising the message.

There are three basic types of evangelism. The first is relational or lifestyle evangelism. Out of our everyday relationships with friends, relatives, acquaintances, and work associates, we share the gospel with them. However, many Christians do not practice this and are not effective at it, especially in these difficult anti-Christian cultures. It is, as R.C. Sproul has said, they are not clear on the gospel. The second is Servant evangelism. We serve others as Christ served us. We express the love of God by caring for them and doing acts of kindness or grace towards them. We help other people with their concerns and also somehow let them know that we have the love of God shed in our hearts for them and perhaps get an opportunity to share the gospel or build bridges that may be crossed later. It is simply caring for our fellowmen. We extend grace and balance that with an invitation to respond to God and his love for them in Christ. The third kind of evangelism is confrontational or what I like to call taking the initiative or direct, intentional evangelism. This is evangelism that may involve giving out a tract, even walking with a sign, explaining the gospel in the park, street one to one evangelism or preaching, or taking the initiative to tell others about the gospel in Christ Jesus.[3] It is taking the initiative to share the gospel. (Mark 2:4; Matthew 5:24; John 21) We take the initiative in business, in finding a job in developing relationships in marriage; why then wouldn't we take the initiative in sharing the gospel. "For the sons of this world are more shrewd in dealing with their own generation than the sons of light" (Luke 16:8). God takes the initiative with us, should we not do likewise with others. Jesus said, "Freely you have received, freely give" (Matthew 10:8, NKJV). We must organize even better than the world to reach the lost, minister to the saved and the unsaved, and do the work of the ministry. "He gave the apostles, the prophets, the evangelists, the shepherds, and teachers, to equip the saints for the work of the ministry, for building up the body of Christ" (Ephesians 4:11-12). These people do the work of ministry and equip other disciples to also do the work of ministry.

Lately, I have been sharing the gospel with people in the city park. I am with a group called the Fellowship of Christian Farmers

Canada. This group is also throughout the United States. We give out walking sticks and share the gospel using the colored bead presentation first begun by C.H. Spurgeon. It is surprising how receptive people are and how many are willing to pray the sinner's prayer after the gospel is clearly presented. There are also other good presentations of the gospel that can be used to present the gospel clearly to people in a rush to go nowhere. (Habakkuk 2:2) The point is we should have a clear presentation available so that we can concisely share the gospel who are in a hurry to go nowhere or anywhere or where they think they have something more important to do than their eternal destiny. "Write the vision; make it plain on tablets, so he may run who reads it" (Habakkuk 2:2).

Not everyone is ready to do confrontation or direct evangelism. As we grow in experiencing the love of God in our hearts, it will overcome any fear and selfishness. We will be thrust into the harvest field. (Matthew 9:38) Many are not even able to share the gospel with their friends because they fear rejection because the gospel confronts man in their sin and lets them know that in their own goodness they cannot go to heaven, and this offends many people. There is also now a strong anti-Christian sentiment. However, the good news is that God has made a way for us to go to heaven and to go there when we must humbly receive the gift of God in Jesus Christ. This gift also involves the fulness of life. Although all of us may not at this time be ready to do confrontational evangelism, all can do some kind of service ministry. However, there are many ways to support this kind of ministry and to be involved supportively.

People give all kinds of excuses for not sharing the gospel because they are afraid. Afraid of rejection and, worse yet, mockery or of being ostracized. We also may be indifferent to the lost and want only to stay in our comfort zone. Some could care less or care more about remaining in their zone of comfort. "Sometimes we make an excuse for remaining silent and not proclaiming the gospel to people, saying: "I'm not going to push my views on others verbally. I'll wait until they respond to my stellar example." We also must admit that few of us are so far along in our sanctification that the world is knocking on our door, asking what makes us so special and begging us to tell them how to get it."[4] We have been way too passive in our evangelism.

Here also is a common misunderstanding, stated again by R.C. Sproul. "In the New Testament, there is a difference between evangelism and witnessing. Christians today tend to use the term witness as a synonym for the verb evangelize as if they were interchangeable. To bear witness to Christ is to call attention to Him in many different ways. We do it by the example that we seek to set with godly living. We seek to bear witness or to make manifest the presence of Christ through deeds and acts of mercy: by feeding the hungry, giving shelter to the homeless, and participating in other charitable endeavors. Those are different kinds of witnessing, but they are not all evangelism. Evangelism is one form of witnessing, but not all witnessing is evangelism. We bear witness to the lordship of Christ in many ways, one of which is the *proclamation* of the gospel."[5] Every Christian is to proclaim the gospel, not just the preacher.

Evangelism is one way we do good works, acts of mercy are another and certainly, forgiveness is at the top. If we experience the heart of God in contemplative prayer, we will care for what he cares for and he primarily cares for the lost, and that is displayed on the cross. (Matthew 18:10-14) J.C. Ryle said, "Others may think it enough to mourn over dead bodies. For my part, I think there is far more cause to mourn over dead souls." The best way to do evangelism is from the heart of Christ put into action. "Whoever, says he is in the light and hates his brother is still in the darkness. Whoever loves his brother abides in the light, and in him, there is no cause for stumbling" (John 2:9). We can express hate but ignoring people and depriving people of Christ.

Of course, not everyone is open to the gospel or open at the time we would like them to be. We, like God, do not force Jesus on people or try to manipulate them. It truly is a work of God and people in the world must pray to God for the gift of faith and repentance and become earnest seekers.

Being a contemplative is a person who lives a dedicated life of prayer. This will lead to loving others from our pure hearts because our love for God has been purified. We will love ourselves with a rightly ordered love, centered in the person and power of Jesus Christ, and with a right ordered love, we love others. This will lead to ministering to others. Every Christian makes a choice to step into ministry. Not necessarily a full-time ministry like a pastor or other, but an attitude of ministry to Christ and others. We will dedicate our money and resources to the Lord's work and the building up of churches because Jesus is the head of the church and has chosen the church as his method to extend the Kingdom of God in people's lives and in the world. Missions will also be a passion of ours and we will seek to spread the gospel to the whole world. (Acts 1:8) We will also care for the poor and those going through hardship. Part of picking up the cross and following Jesus is stepping into a ministry to others. It is not just being concerned and responsible for our own little world, but for the lives of others. We will also assist fellow Christians to be all they can be in Christ.

We will disciple others to follow Christ and assist them to grow as we also continue to grow. (Matthew 28:18-20) This is especially important for new Christians. We need a new Christian class in our churches and people that will walk with others in friendship and discipleship to help them grow. People can be mentored, coached, counseled, and when they are ready, to be assisted with planned education in spiritual formation and spiritual direction. We can come alongside people and help them to grow in Christ-likeness and prayer. If we care for God's people, we will be part of the process and they will be fed spiritually. (John 21:17) Jesus came down from the mountain with Peter, James, and John and cast out demons. This is also a ministry of the church in those rare occurrences and those for very spiritually mature, gifted, and those centered well in Christ.

The contemplative life and the active life go together. Sometimes we may focus on the contemplative, but it will lead us, in time to the active life. The closer we grow in love with God and for God, the more we will experience healing, spiritually, psychologically, and if it is His will, physically. However, through the process, we can learn to trust him. In his book Ruthless Trust, Brennan Manning tells the story of a man's encounter with Mother Teresa. The man traveled thousands of miles to talk to her and ask her to pray for him. The man said when asked by her, "Pray that I have clarity." She said firmly, "No, I will not do that." When he asked her why, she said, "Clarity is the last thing you are clinging to and must let go of." When Kavanaugh commented that she always seemed to have the clarity he longed for, she laughed and said, "I have never had clarity; what I have always had is trust. So, I will pray that you trust God."[6] God is often leading us and the hardest matter is to trust God and step out in faith. (Proverbs 3:5-6)

One day I was driving in the Palm Springs area and saw a man with a billboard that stated that Jesus was coming back soon. I thought to myself that this is probably not very effective. However, it seemed like the Spirit spoke to my mind and said, "At least he is doing something." Something for Jesus and with Jesus. If we love Jesus, we will find a way to tell others and it may mean many times of not being seemingly very effective, but where there is a will, there is a way. We can learn to be effective, but as C.H. Spurgeon said, "We are not responsible to God for the soul that is saved, but we are responsible for the Gospel that is preached, and for the way in which we preach it." We are just to be faithful to the message and leave the results to God.

We can find a way to minister in the church and in the world. (Matthew 25:31-40) We can tell others about Jesus and if we don't give up, we will find a way that works for us. We are part of the Jesus team and we have a place where we can contribute finan-cially, with hospitality, with our hearts, hands, and feet. We all have spiritual gifts and if we act from our heart, we will, in the process, discover those gifts, as they will rise to the top. We can find a place to serve and the gifts will take care of themselves. The contemplative life and the active life must be held in balance, but the active life will truly come out of the contemplative life.

CHAPTER 16

FOCUS AND DISCERNMENT

When we walk in the fulness of the image of God— we walk in our true self in Christ. The Apostle John had his identity in Christ, he referred to himself as the "disciple whom Jesus loved." (John 20:2) If we do not walk in our full self as much as possible in this life, we will not glorify God to the full extent. Jesus said that he and "the Father are one." (John 10:30) In one sense, Jesus was one with the Father in a way we cannot. He was a part of the Trinity. He is God. In another sense, we can be one with the Father as Jesus is. Jesus was one with the Father in purpose, in desire, in love and action and will. We can be as well. This is the universal and ultimate calling of men and women.

The Bible records the event of Mary in Martha in Luke 10:38-42. Martha was getting the meal ready and was "distracted with much serving." Mary was sitting at the feet of Jesus, enthralled with him and learning with great attentiveness and devotion to Jesus. Martha somewhat curtly says, "Lord, do you not care that my sister has left me to serve alone." Jesus says, "one thing is necessary." Mary was sitting at the feet of Jesus, expressing faith and submission to his greatness, beauty, and teaching. She expressed a readiness to believe and served him with her attentiveness. Her focus at the moment was on Jesus, he was the priority. His teaching and his presence were desired above all other things and people. He was desired even above food.

This doesn't mean that we are not to serve by our actions, as we mentioned in the Contemplative and active life, but it does mean that spending time with Jesus in quality-focused time in prayer is the one thing that is necessary above everything else. Mary expressed her love to Jesus by being entrenched in what he was about. She was enjoying being with Jesus. Jesus comes before everyone else and everything else. He is Lord and it is good to recognize this by our words, actions, and attitudes. We need to make Jesus through prayer our first and foremost priority. This is the time best spent. As Jesus stated, "One thing is necessary" (Luke 10:42).

Jesus said, "You, therefore, must be perfect, as your heavenly Father is perfect" (Matthew 5:48). As Oswald Chambers has said, "Every man is made to reach out beyond his grasp."[1] Spiritual perfection is the goal, although, in this life, we will never reach it and we will never reach it in our own strength. It, however, allows for no excuses and will, in the end, move us continually towards the upward call of God in Christ Jesus. (Philippians 3:14) We will, if this is our goal and calling, continue to strive to realize our utmost for His glory. This only occurs as we progress in prayer with God. Prayer is at the heart of our relationship with the Lord.

The glory of God in our life is God's ultimate purpose for us. Anything less and we will be settling for less than life. John Piper has wrestled with and has some great teaching on the glory of God, although I would be careful with some of his statements. He says, "Does Christian Hedonism put man's pleasure above God's glory. No. It put man's pleasure in God's glory. Our quest is not merely joy. It is joy in God."[2] Yes, if we have rightly ordered self-love, we will desire the fulness of God in Jesus Christ, but our focus must never be self, but God. Yes, joy is the result of being close to God and therefore glorifying Him, but our object is not our joy but God and His holiness—a purified love for himself, not for just our own benefit. If we don't love him fully, we will never fathom the cross nor pick it up. We really don't know love unless we know God and know him in his fulness. (1 John 4:8) The greater is our purified love for God, the greater God is in our lives and we can, like will Jesus, endure the cross (persecution) because of the joy set before us. (Hebrews 12:2) He is our joy. Jesus loved the Father and wanted to please him and the Father was pleased with Jesus. (Matthew 3:17) We please those we love.

God came humbly to us as a child in a manager. Jesus is God in the flesh. (John 1:14; Philippians 2:1-11) He set a beautiful example even though he is God by coming humbly and those who come to him must come humbly. Jacques Philippe said, "No joy can compare with the joy tasted by those who are truly poor in spirit."[3] Those who recognize mankind's poverty. Those who recognize their ultimate need and dependence on God for anything, especially anything good. (Philippians 1:27; 4:8)

Malcolm Muggeridge calls the phrase "the pursuit of happiness" in our American Declaration of Independence one of the silliest things ever said."[4] If we pursue happiness as our goal, it will be little trying to grasp air in our hands. However, if we pursue God and his holiness, we will find happiness. We might have to endure some hardship, but the end will be more than worth it. When Peter, James, and John went with Jesus to the mount of transfiguration, they were at first terrified to see Jesus lifted up in the air together with Moses and Elijah. The brilliance of their beings was hard to gaze upon. After their initial shock and they absorbed his beauty beyond all comprehension as Peter expressed that he just wanted to stay with Jesus on the Mount. We likewise are initially shocked at looking at our corruption, but if we humbly stay before God in repentance, we will experience his healing and transformation. "In this peaceful refreshment, the soul attains the rest in God it seeks, however many obstacles block its path. Countless are the seductive ways of the world, the wiles of the devil, the futile attempts we make to put the pride form, not the Christ form, at the center of our life."[5]

Consider what John of the Cross so succinctly says, "The soul must practice the following instructions if it wishes to attain in a short time holy recollection and spiritual silence, nakedness, and poverty of spirit, where one enjoys the peaceful and comfort of the Holy Spirit, reaches union with God, is freed of all the obstacles incurred from the creatures of this world, defended against the wiles of the devil and liberated from one's own self."[6]

Unless we develop a life of prayer on this earth, we will miss out on what is most valuable—the fulness of God. Prayer is communion with God and it is the way God uses to develop a quality relationship with us and transform us so we can accept his fullness. We must go on to experience contemplative prayer, even though it is a gift from God, and learn to walk in the way of spiritual formation. Unless we do, we walk in less than fulness and leave ourselves venerable to the influence of the evil one.

Those who are big on control might find prayer quite difficult. There is a mystery in God and it is truly experienced in prayer. "In prayer, there is a mystery that absolutely surpasses our understanding."[7] Those who overemphasize the head and dangerously think they know God, just in their intellect, are greatly lacking. We must know God in our head as well as our heart, not to mention even our will and purified memory, as Saint John of the cross mentions. Today we might call purified memory the healing of memories

"Dr. Tozer, writing somewhat later from America, makes a moving summons to evangelical Christians to seek a deeper relationship with the Lord Himself, to know Him more and be with Him in prayer.

In our day, everything is made to center upon the initial act of "accepting" Christ (a term, incidentally, which is not found in the Bible) and we are not expected thereafter to crave any further revelation of God in our souls. We have been snared in the coils of a spurious logic that insists that if we have found Him, we need no more seek him. This is set before us as the last word in orthodoxy, and it is taken for granted that no Bible taught Christian ever believed otherwise... In the midst of this great chill, there are some I rejoice to acknowledge who will not be content with shallow logic. They will admit the force of the argument and turn away with tears to hunt some lonely place and pray, "Oh God, show me thy glory." They want to taste, to touch with their hearts, to see with their inner eyes the wonder that is God."[8]

Those who have been the primary stewards of spiritual theology and the complete and progressive process of sanctification have been the Catholics. They have been the ones that have seen the value of the interior life and the purgation of the heart—the desires of mankind. "Charles Simpson, a Baptist minister, seems to say it best.

"One of the contrasts we've noticed in our contacts with Catholics in the charismatic renewal is the emphasis lacking in most Protestant circles. Catholics generally emphasize the whole process of salvation, whereas Protestants, at least my kind, tend to emphasize the initial new birth. The two truths, which have been kept isolated for so long, need to be taken together. If we see all of Christianity as being wrapped up in the new birth, we miss (I'll use a word we don't use often) the sacramental aspects of the fellowship of the Church. If we don't get the starting point, we might think we can grow in the Church without getting plugged in spiritually. Both truths are needed for the Church to be what it needs to be. The Catholic tradition tends to produce a few spiritual giants, the evangelical tradition produces a lot of spiritual babies. We need babies, a lot of them if the Church is to grow, but those babies need to grow up and reproduce themselves if the Church is going to be real. We have to take the two truths together."[9]

The Charismatics have been a blessing in the reliance and emphasis on the Holy Spirit. However, they are not, for the most part, familiar with the process that God has for us in the transformation that occurs in contemplative prayer, although they are people of prayer. The focus is primarily on experience rather than

God himself. We are not to seek God primarily for experiences but primarily for himself. "Therefore, careful and informed spiritual direction is essential if the charismatic movement is to make progress. The movement needs to create within it a network of spiritual guides who can help individuals through peak experiences and enable them to cope with the inevitable experience of darkness for which traditional Pentecostal spirituality may leave them unprepared."[10]

All men and women have a longing within. The longing is often mistaken, but the longing is for God. He is our center, our light, our home, our fulness, our life. We are not content unless we find our home. Some people nurture this longing and others deny it and squelch it, for God does not force himself on anyone. What are we doing to get in touch with the longing and let it come to fruition? We can pray, read our Bible, and read spiritual and Theological books. We can fellowship with others; we are also in touch with this longing and join with Christ in a local church. We can also tell others about the gospel. Can we be fishermen and not fish. Jesus said, "Follow me and I will make you fishers of men" (Matthew 4:19)

Jesus is calling you to life. Life by being born again spiritually. Life through His spirit and fullness of life as we progress with life in the spirit in prayer. If we don't make much room in our life for God in prayer and otherwise, we will miss out on life's greatest blessing and on the rewards that are there for us in heaven. Nothing and no one can stop you from growing spiritually. No circumstance can stop you; no person can stop you—you, in God's strength, can overcome. The Apostle Paul wrote Ephesians, Philippians, Colossians, and Philemon while in jail because of his preaching of the gospel. Later he was put to death. Nothing stopped Paul. It is one matter to suffer justly for the wrong you have done; it is another to suffer patiently and spiritually for the wrongs committed against you. As the scriptures state, "Who shall separate us from the love of Christ? Shall tribulation, or distress, or persecution, or famine, or nakedness, or danger, or sword: As it is written: For your sake, we are being killed all the day long; we are regarded as sheep to be slaughtered" (Romans 8:35-36) This is love. This is dedication. This is faithfulness. This is finding what is of great value and being loyal to him.

If our life is rightly ordered, we will find fulfillment. If it is disordered, it will result in emptiness and destruction. When our heart is purified, we will love others out of pure love, not a love contaminated by inordinate self-love. The more we are hurt, the more we protect ourselves and look after number one. Many who have been hurt or hurt others live with a despised self and try to survive and cover it up with an illusion of self to get by. They are constantly in their self-talk, putting themselves down and accepting negative and often distorted thoughts about themselves. Some thoughts come right from the evil one. Both those that love themselves too much and those that hate themselves need to come to Christ for healing. He will set us free. Free to be real, free to be our true selves in Jesus Christ and fulfill our destiny and calling. His offer is always with his provision and strength. We must step out in faith; we must become and stay people of prayer—loyal to the one who is love and we will enjoy that love.

The beautiful thing is the Trinity invites us to a loving fellowship with him. This is the greatest invitation. God affirms you and extends his love to you in this invitation. This invitation does you no good unless you and I accept it. He invites us to eternal life in conversion and invites us to the fulness of life. (Ephesians 3:19)

As God's word says, "I call heaven and earth to witness against you today, that I have set before you life ad death, blessings and curse. Therefore, choose life, that you and your descendants might live" (Deuteronomy 30:19)

The Greatest blessing in this life is eternal life in and through Jesus Christ. The greatest blessing for the Christian is a life of prayer and the spiritual formation that occurs in prayer that closely connects us with the living God and we are transformed in co-operating with Him and allowing Him to conform us to His image miraculously within. This only occurs as we advance in our relationship with God in and through prayer. Prayer is something anyone can do. He is readily available. Learn to pray by praying. At first, it will be difficult, and you will be attacked by many distractions. Focus on God, ask him to purify you, ask him to strengthen you. Ask him to give you the most marvelous gift of contemplative prayer.

God bless you in your journey. He wants to bless us more than we can think or imagine. "Now to him who is able to do far more abundantly than all we ask or think, according to the power at work within us" (Ephesians 3:20). Look to him and find your enjoyment and fulfillment in him and his glory. We can enjoy being with God by living a life of prayer. God enjoys being with us. "God does not have his favorites, but he does have his intimates."[11] We all can be one of his intimates. God invites us to himself. Are you willing to put in the effort, as God does his work in you, and as you make yourself available to him?

CONCLUSION

The Westminster Shorter Catechism says, "Man's chief end is to glorify God and enjoy him forever." The way we primarily glorify God is to reflect His glory in Christlikeness and enjoy Him. When we enjoy God, we are truly entering into God and enjoying his goodness, his holiness, his love, and his peace. There is also the enjoyment of having faith in Him. "There is a peace the world cannot give (cf. Jn. 14:27), a level of peace I cannot control at will." [1]

God invites us to the greatest enjoyment and that is Him. For anyone else to say, this would be very egotistical and illusionary. He is the greatest enjoyment because he is the essence of goodness, love, truth, justice, and grace. He is everything that is good and to be united to him is to be united and to experience what is "very good." (Genesis 1:31) "By means of this mystical theology and secret love, the soul departs from itself and all things and ascends to God." [2] "Besides its usual effect, this mystical wisdom will occasionally so engulf a person in its secret abyss that he will have a keen awareness of being brought into a place far removed from every creature." [3] This is a work of God because God is the great initiator.

The enjoyment is the occasional experience and or progressive experience of heaven on earth--entering into God and his fulness. Nothing is more enjoyable, but so few find it in fulness. "For many are called, but few chosen" (Matthew 22:14). This relates to salvation, but also, as the Apostle Paul calls it, to our "holy calling" in Christ Jesus. (2 Timothy 1:9)

The invitation is to come, to come and enjoy God. John the Apostle refers to himself as the "disciple whom Jesus loved." At the last supper, John "was reclining at table at Jesus side for he was so enthralled in love with Jesus and wanted to be close to him. We can be close to him as well. He invites us to come. Jesus said, "Come to me, all you who labor and are heavily laden, and I will give you rest" (Matthew 11:28). God's rest is the fulness of life in Jesus Christ.

Enjoy Being with God as He enjoys being with you. He is the greatest enjoyment of this life and the life to come. "Though our outer self is wasting away, our inner self is being renewed day by day (2 Corinthians 4:16).

Enjoy that Lord in hardship and in victory, as did the Apostle Paul. Even in suffering in Christ, there are consolations. (2 Corinthians 1:1-7) God's will is good and if we enjoy the goodness, we will enjoy doing his will with a purified heart to his glory. (2 Corinthians 3:7-11) "Whether God consoles us or withholds any sign of affection ought not to make a difference. It is better to embrace a bitterness of a desert experience, in which a profound inner purification may be happening than to run to an oasis of old comforts."[4]

Enjoying God in his fullness comes about through a life of contemplative prayer. We enjoy him in his fullness and live in it, in full union with him in practice. When we live in close intimate union with God in Christ, we can love him and enjoy him and then become like Him. All that is beautiful, all that is good, all that is true love in fullness, all that is just, and righteousness is in him and he infuses into us his goodness and we can live in his glory as God planned for us from the beginning. Like we enjoy him in heaven, we can enjoy him now, in spite of circumstances and because of them. He is our great joy and fulfillment.

We have the great privilege of enjoying God. This inheritance is available to all Christians, it is inherent in our calling. It is the fulness of life Jesus invites us to. It is the rivers of living water welling up in our hearts. These waters give life and give life abundantly. "To the thirsty, I will give from the spring of the water of life without payment" (Revelation 21:6). We can enjoy life and life abundantly in him. This fulfillment is found in spending quality time with God in prayer and thus being formed in his full image in Christ. The greatest good is to enjoy God and thus glorify Him. It is to enter fully as far as possible in this life the fulness of God in and through Jesus Christ. To Him be the glory, honor, and praise.

Enter into the full enjoyment of God and enter into the full enjoyment of God in heaven. Enter into His rest. (Hebrews 4:1-11)

The End.

Notes

Preface

1. Gordon T. Smith, *Teach Us to Pray*, (Dowers Grove, Illinois: IVP Books, 2018) 1.

Introduction

1. Christopher Lasch, *The Culture of Narcissism*, (New York, N.Y.: W.W.Norton & Co.,1979)
2. Eugene Peterson, *Christ Plays in Ten Thousand Places*, (Grand Rapids: Eerdmans Publishing, 2205) 1.
3. Susan Muto, *Words of Wisdom for Our World: The Precautions and Counsels of St. John of the Cross*, (Washington, DC.: ICS Publications, 1996) 50.
4. St. John of the Cross, *The Collected Works of St. John of the Cross*, trans. Kieran Kavanaugh, Otilio Rodriguez, (ICS Publications: Washington, D.C.,1991) 507
5. Ryan Denton, *Ten Modern Myths: A Biblical Corrective*, (Grand Rapids: Reformation Heritage Books, 2021) p.14
6. Ibid, p.22, cited from, J.I. Packer, *Evangelism and the Sovereignty of God*, 41
7. Muto, Words of Wisdom for Our World, 60
8. Ibid,30.
9. Thomas Merton, *Sign of Jonas*, 236 cited in Muto, *Words of Wisdom for Our World*, 61

1. Full Union with God in Christ

1. Kavanaugh, *The Collected Works of St. John of the Cross*, 387.
2. James Houston, *The Transforming Power of Prayer*, (Colorado Springs: NavPress, 1996) 195.

2. A SAINT-One who is in Christ

1. Ibid, 23.
2. Muto, *Words of Wisdom*, 27
3. Houston, *The Transforming Power of Prayer*, 23.
4. Ibid, 105.

3. The Missing Blessing

1. D. Bruce Hindmarsh, The Spirit of Early Evangelicalism: True Religion in the Modern World, (New York, NY: Oxford University Press, 2018, 181.
2. Thomas Dubay, Fire Within, (San Francisco: Ignatius Press,1989),86.
3. Houston, The Transforming Power of Prayer, 290.
4. Ibid, 16.
5. Ibid,15.
6. Houston, The Transforming Power of Prayer, 271.
7. Ibid, 255.

4. Our Heritage

1. Houston, The Transforming Power of Prayer, 192.
2. Inst. 3.25.10. cited in Michael Horton, Justification, vol 2, (Grand Rapids: Zondervan,2018) 488.
3. Maximus the Confessor, Ambigua, 41, trans. Vishnevskay, "Divinization and Spiritual Progress, "141, Cited in David Meconi and Carl E. Olson, Called to Be Children of God, (San Francisco: Ignatius Press, 2016) 53.
4. James Houston, "Spirituality," Evangelical Dictionary of Theology, ed. Walter A. Elwood (Grand Rapids: Baker, 1984, 105. Cited in Bruce Demarest, Satisfy Your Soul, (Colorado Springs, NavPress,1999) 167.
5. Tom Schwanda, Soul Recreation: The Contemplative-Mystical Piety of Puritanism, (Eugene, Oregon: Pickwick Publications, 2021) 231
6. Ibid, 222.
7. Ibid,119.
8. Ibid, 121.
9. Newman, Parochial and Plain Sermons, 7:86, Cited in, David Meconi and Carl E. Olson, Called to Be Children of God, 194.
10. Houston, The Transforming Power of Prayer, 17.
11. Richard Foster, Freedom of Simplicity, (San Francisco: Harper & Row Publishers,1971,1973)

5. Sanctification Positionally and Practically in Christ

1. Matthew Mead, Almost Christian Discovered, (Reformation Heritage Books, 1993)
2. Kenneth L. Chafin, Mastering the New Testament, 1,2 Corinthians, (USA, Word, Incorperated, 1985) 25.
3. Michael Molinos, The Spiritual Guide, (Sargent, GA: Seed Sowers, 1983),63.
4. Iain H. Murray, Spurgeon vs. Hyper-Calvinism, (Edinburgh: Banner of Truth, 2000) 18
5. Thomas, John Paul. The Mystical Journey to Divine Union: Spiritual Wisdom from Saint John of the Cross, (My Catholic Life: 2018) 12
6. Ralph Martin, Hungry for God, (Garden City, New York: Doubleday & Co.,1974) 56.

7. Mead, *The Almost Christian Discovered*, 81.
8. Jim Manney, *What Do You Really Want?* (USA, Jim Maney, Publisher, 2015),27.
9. Raymond B. Dillard, *Faith in the Face of Apostasy*, (Phillipsburg, New Jersey, P&R Publishing, 1999),46.

6. The Overview of the Process of Spiritual Formation

1. Jacques Philippe, *Thirsting for Prayer*, (Rochelle, NY: Scepter, 2014) p.16

7. Types of Prayer

1. Michael Molinos, *The Spiritual Guide*, 5.
2. Willian A. Barry & William J. Connolly, *The Practise of Spiritual Direction*, (New York: Seabury Press, 1982), 49.
3. Kavanaugh, *The Collected Works of St. John of the Cross*, 356.

8. Reaching the Heights

1. Benedicta Ward & Norman Russell, *The Lives of the Desert Fathers*, (Trappist, Kentucky: Cistercian publishers, 1980)
2. Athanasius, *The Life of Antony and the Letter of Marcellinus*, (New Jersey: Paulist Press,1980)
3. Jacques Philippe, Thirsting for Prayer, 53.
4. Thomas, *The Mystical Journey to Divine Union*,.153.
5. Kavanaugh, *The Collected Works of Saint John of the Cross*, 14.

9. Stages Along the Way

1. Ibid, p. 77.
2. Ralph Martin, *The Fulfillment of All Desire: A Guidebook for the Journey to God, Based on the Wisdom of the Saints,* (Steubenville, Ohio: Emmaus Road Publishing,2006)
3. Trans. C.E. Rolt, *Dionysius the Areopagite on the Divine Names and The Mystical Theology*, (Berwick, Maine: Ibis Press, 2004)
4. David Hubbard, *Preachers Commentary on Proverbs*, (Nashville, Tennessee: Thomas Nelson, 2018.
5. Norbert Cummins, *Freedom to Rejoice*, (London: Harper-Collins Publishers, 1991)10
6. Keith R. Anderson & Randy D. Reese, *Spiritual Mentoring*, (Downers Grove, Illinois: IVP Books,1999) p.103.
7. Francis Kelly Nemeck & Marie Theresa Coombs, *The Way of Spiritual Direction*, (Collegeville, Minnesota: The Liturgical Press, 1985) p.69.

8. Complied by St. Nikodimos of the Holy Mountain, trans. By G.F.H. Palmer, Philp Sherrard, Kallistos Ware, *The Philokalia,* (London, Boston: Faber and Faber, vol. 1, 1979) p.325.
9. Muto, *Words of Wisdom for our World,* 49.
10. Thomas, *The Mystical Journey to Divine Union,* 93
11. Ibid, 127
12. Green, *When the Well Runs Dry,* (Notre Dame, Indiana: Ave Maria Press, 2002) 39.
13. Ibid, 94
14. Cummins, *Freedom to Rejoice,* 31
15. Ibid, 19.
16. Ibid
17. Ibid, 56.
18. Green, *When the Well Runs Dry,* 27.
19. Thomas H. Green, Weeds Among the Wheat, (Notre Dame, Indiana: Ave Maria Press, 2005) 125
20. Thomas H. Green, *Drinking From a Dry Well,* (Notre Dame, Indiana: Ave Maria Press, 1990) 51
21. Ibid, 15
22. Bernard of Clairvaux, Selected Works: The Classics of Western Spirituality, (New York: Paulist Press, 1987) 192
23. D.A. Carons, *Divine Sovereignty, and Human Responsibility,* (Eugene, Oregon: Wipf and Stock Publishers, 1994)
24. J.I. Packer, Evangelism and the Sovereignty of God, (Downers Grove, Illinois: Inter-Varsity Press, 1971) 35-36.
25. Philippe, *Thirsting for Prayer,* 2.
26. Thomas, *The Mystical Journey of the Divine Union,* 91.
27. Ibid, 7
28. Thomas, *The Mystical Journey of the Divine Union,* 16.
29. Ibid, .72.
30. Tom Schwanda, *Soul Recreation,*
31. Trans. Kieran Kavanaugh & Otilio Rodriguez, *St. Teresa of Avila, vol. 2,* (Washington, D.C.: ICS Publications, 1980)
32. Keith Anderson & Randy Reese, *Spiritual Mentoring,* 113.
33. John Piper, *Desiring God,* (Sisters, Oregon: Multnomah Publishers, 1986) 28
34. Bruce Demarest, *Satisfy Your Soul,* (Colorado Spring, Co.: NavPress, 1999)30.
35. Muto, Words of Wisdom for our World, 51.

10. ATTACHMENTS

1. Cummins, *Freedom to Rejoice,* 7.
2. The Philokalia, vol. 2, St. Theodoros the Great Ascetic, 34.
3. Thomas, *The Mystical Journey of the Divine Union,* 50.
4. Isaac Ambrose, *Looking to Jesus,* ed. William Kritlow, 2021. Vol.1,2,3.
5. Cummins, *Freedom to Rejoice,* 23
6. Richard Foster, *Freedom of Simplicity,* (New York: Harper & Row Pulblishers,1981)
7. Ralph C. Martin, *Called to Holiness,* (Ann Arbor, Michigan: Servant Books, 188) 119.

8. Richard Foster, *Celebration of Discipline*, (San Francisco: Harper, 1978,1988,1999)
9. Keith Anderson, 123.
10. Thomas, The *Mystical Journey of the Divine Union*, 29.

11. CONSOLATION AND DESOLATION

1. Craig R. Koester, *Revelation and the End of All Things*, (Grand Rapids, Michigan: Eerdmans, 2001) 86.
2. Timothy M. Gallagher, *Discernment of Spirits*, (New York: Crossroad Publishing Co., 2005)
3. Gordon T. Smith, *Teach Us to Pray*, 85.
4. Thomas H. Green, *Weeds Among Thorns*, (Notre Dame, IN: Ave Maria Press, 2005) 108
5. Gordon T. Smith, *Listening to God in Times of Choice*, (Downers Grove, Illinois: Intervarsity Press), 1997
6. Ibid, 86-88

12. DARK NIGHT OF THE SOUL

1. Jurgen Moltmann, The Crucified God, (Minneapolis: Fortress Press, 1993) 55.
2. Cummins, *Freedom to Rejoice*, 145.
3. Ibid, 168
4. Keith R. Anderson and Randy D. Reese, *Spiritual Mentoring*, 118.
5. Cummins, *Freedom to Rejoice*, 169.
6. Ibid, 49.
7. Ibid, 89.
8. Kavanaugh, *The Collected Works of St. John of the Cross*, 197.
9. Ibid, 118.
10. Ibid, 405.
11. Phillipe, *Thirsting for Prayer*, 10.
12. Anderson, *Spiritual Mentoring*, 117.

13. THE CONTEMPLATIVE LIFE

1. Raymond B. Dillard, *Faith in the Face of Apostasy*, 55.
2. Thomas H. Green, *When the Well Runs Dry*, 19.
3. Ibid, 29.

14. THE CONTEMPLATIVES THAT HAVE GONE BEFORE US

1. Cummins, *Freedom to Rejoice*, 6.
2. Evelyn Underhill, *Mysticism*, (New York, Dutton & Co., Inc, 1961) xiv.

3. Jeanne Guyon, *Experiencing the Depths of Jesus Christ*, (Jacksonville, FL: Seed-Sowers Publishing, MCMLXXV) back cover.
4. A.W. Tozer, *The Pursuit of God*, (Harrisburg, Penn: Christian Publications, 1982),50.
5. Green, *When the Well Runs Dry*, 27.
6. Michael Molinos, *The Spiritual Guide*, 71.
7. Green, *When the Well Runs Dry*, 19.
8. Cited in, David Meconli and Carl E. Olson, *Called to be Children of God*, (San Francisco, Ignatius Press, 2016) 103. Peter D. Fehler, The Role of Charity in the Ecclesiology of St. Bonaventure, Selecta Seraphina, 2 (Rome: Editrice Miscellanea Francescana, 1965) 78.
9. Houston, *The Transforming Power of Prayer*,241.
10. Martin Luther, *Lectures on Romans*, in LW 25:267. Cited in, Michael Horton, *Justification, vol. 2*,(Grand Rapids: Zondervan, 2018) 457

15. The Active Life

1. R.C. Sproul, *what is the Gospel?* Reformation Trust Publishing, 2020, 1-2.
2. Ibid, 11
3. Ryan Denton, *Ten Modern Evangelism Myths: A Biblical Corrective*, (Grand Rapids, Michigan: Reformation Heritage Books, 2021) 37-39
4. Ibid, 104
5. Ibid, 104
6. Brennan Manning, *Ruthless Trust*, (Harper One, 2000) 5

16. Focus and Discernment

1. Oswald Chambers, *My Utmost for His Highest*, (Uhrichville, Ohio: Barbour Publishing, 1935,1963) Dec.22
2. John Piper, *Desiring God*, 306.
3. Philippe, *Thirsting for Prayer*, 60.
4. Peter Kreeft, *Making Sense Out of Suffering*, (Ann Arbor, Michigan: Servant Books, 1986) 143.
5. Susan Muto, *Words of Wisdom for Today*, 27.
6. Ascent of Mount Carmel. Bk.1 chap. 13. See11, from the Collected Works of St. John of the Cross, trans. Kieran Kavanaugh and Otilio Rodriquez, rev. ed. (Washington, DC: ICS Publications, 1991).
7. Jacques Philippe, *Thirsting for Prayer*, 7.
8. Ralph Martin, *Hungry for God*, 27.
9. Ibid, 29
10. Kenneth Leech, Soul Friend, (San Francisco: Harper and Row, Publishers, 1977) 32
11. Demarest, Satisfy Your Soul, 103.

Conclusion

1. Susan Muto, *Words of Wisdom for our World*, 26.
2. Cummins, *Freedom to Rejoice*, 160.
3. Ibid, 166.
4. Muto, *Words of Wisdom for Our World*, 58.

BIBLIOGRAPHY

Ambrose Isaac, *Looking to Jesus*, USA: William Kritlow, 2021.

Anderson R. Keith & Reese D. Randy, *Spiritual Mentoring*, Downers Grove, Illinois: IVP Books, 1999.

Athanasius, *The Life of Antony & Letter of Marcellinus*, New Jersey: Paulist Press, 1980

Barry William A. & Connolly William J., *The Practice of Spiritual Direction*, New York: The Seabury Press, 1982.

Carson, D.A., *Divine Sovereignty and Human Responsibility*, Eugene Oregon: Wipf and Stock Publishers, 1994.

Chambers Oswald, *My Utmost for His Highest*, Uhrichville, Ohio: Barbour Publishing, 1935.

Cummins Norbert, *Freedom to Rejoice*, London: Harper Collins Publishers, 1991.

Denton Ryan, *Ten Modern Evangelism Myths*, Grand Rapids: Reformation Heritage Books, 2021.

Demarest Bruce, *Satisfy Your Soul*, Colorado Springs: NavPress, 1999.

---. *Soulguide*, Colorado Springs|: NavPress, 2003.

Dillard Raymond B., *Faith in the Face of Apostasy*, New Jersey: P&R Publishing, 1999.

Dubay Thomas, *Fire Within*, San Francisco: Ignatius Press, 1989.

Foster J. Richard, *Celebration of Discipline*, San Francisco: Harper, 1998.

---. *Freedom of Simplicity*, San Francisco: Harper, 1998.

---. *Sanctuary of the Soul*, Downers Grove, Illinois: InterVarsity Press,2011

Green Thomas H., *When the Well Runs Dry*, Notre Dame, Indiana,2002.

Gallagher Timothy M., *Discernment of Spirits*, New York: Crossway Publishing Co., 2005

---. *Spiritual Consolations*, New York: The Crossroad Publishing Co., 2007.

Hindmarsh, Bruce, D., *The Spirit of Early Evangelicals*, New York: Oxford University Press, 2018.

Ed. Huffman S. Douglas, Henry & Richard Blackaby, Garry Friesen, Gordon T. Smith, *How Then Should We Choose*, Grand Rapids Michigan: Kregel Publications, 2009.

Horton Michael, *Justification, vol. 1 & 2*, Grand Rapids: Zondervan, 2018.

Houston James, *The Transforming Power of Prayer*, Colorado Springs: NavPress, 1996.

---. *The Heart's Desire*, Oxford: A Lion Book, 1992.

---. *The Mentored Life*, Colorado Springs: NavPress, 2002.

Hubbard David, *The Preachers Commentary, vol.15, Proverbs*, Nashville, Tennessee: Thomas Nelson, Inc., 1989.

Trans. Kavanaugh Kieran & Rodriguez Otilio, *St. John of the Cross*, Washington, D.C.: ICS Publications, 1991.

Trans. Kavanaugh Kieran & Rodriguez Otilio, *St. Teresa of Avila, vol. two*, Washington, D.C.: ICS Publications, 1980.

Koester Craig, R., *Revelation and the End of All Things*, Grand Rapids, Michigan: Eerdmans, 2001.

Kreeft Peter, *Making Sense of Suffering*, Ann Arbor, Michigan: Servant Books, 1986.

---. *Happiness and Contemplation*, South Bend, Indiana, 1998.

Lasch Christopher, *Culture of Narcissism*, New York, N.Y., A Warner Communications Co.,1979

Leech Kenneth, *Soul Friend*, Harper and Row Publishers, 1977.

Lisieux St. Therese, *The Story of a Soul*, Rockford Illinois: Tan Books and Publishers, Inc., 1951.

Manning Brennan, *Ruthless Trust*, Harper One, 2005.

Martin Ralph, C., *Hungry for God*, Garden City, NY: Doubleday & Co., 1974.

---. *Called to Holiness*, Ann Arbor, Michigan: Servant Books,1988.

---. *The Fulfillment of All Desire*, Steubenville, Ohio: Emmaus Road Publishing, 2006.

Mead Mathew, *The Almost Christian Discovered*, Reformation Heritage Books, 1993.

Meconi David & Olson Carl E., *Called to Be Children of God*, San Francisco: Ignatius Press, 2016

Molinos Michael, *The Spiritual Guide*, Sargent, Ga: Seedsowers, MCMLXXX11.

Moltmann Jurgen, *The Crucified God*, Minneapolis: Fortress Press, 1993.

Murray Iain H., *Spurgeon vs. Hyper-Calvinism*, Pennsylvania: Banner of Truth, 2000.

Muto Susan, *Words of Wisdom for Our World: The Precautions of St. John of the Cross*, Washington, D.C., ICS Publications, 1995.

Nemeck Francis Kelly & Coombs Marie Theresa, *The Way of Spiritual Direction*, Collegeville, Minnesota: The Liturgical Press, 1985.

Packer J.I., *Evangelism and the Sovereignty of God*, (Downers Grove, Illinois: InterVarsity Press, 1971), 35-36.

Palmer G.F.H, Sherrard Philip, Ware Kallistos, *The Philokalia, vol. 1*, London, Boston: Faber & Faber, 1979.

Peterson Eugene, *Christ Plays in Ten Thousand Places*, Grand Rapids: Eerdmans Publishing, 2005.

Philippe Jacques, *Thirsting for Prayer*, New Rochelle, NY: Scepter Publishing, 2014.

Piper John, *Desiring God*, Sisters Oregon: Multnomah Publishers, 2003.

Trans. Rolt, C.E. *Dionysius the Areopagite on the Divine Names and The Mystical Theology*, Berwick, Maine: Ibis Press, 2004.

Schwanda Tom, *Soul Recreation*, Eugene Oregon: Pickwick Publications, 2021.

Smith T. Gordon, *Teach of to Pray*, Downers Grove, Illinois: IVP Books, 2018.

---. *Listening to God in Times of Choice*, Downers Grove, Illinois: Intervarsity Press, 1997.

Spidlik Tomas, *The Art of Purifying the Heart*, Columbia: Convivium Press, 2010.

Sproul R.C., *What is the Gospel*, China: Reformation Trust Publishing, 2002.

Thomas John Paul, *The Mystical Journey to the Divine Union*, My Catholic Life, 2018.

Ward Benedicta & Russell Norman, *The Lives of the Desert Fathers*, Trappist Kentucky: Cistercian Publishers, 1980.

Manufactured by Amazon.ca
Bolton, ON

27370563R00103